Master the Basics

8 Principles to Growing a Successful Business

By

Dean Williams

Business

Master the Basics

Copyright © 2018: Dean Williams

Published by Conscious Dreams Publishing

www.consciousdreamspublishing.com

Edited by Rhoda Molife, Molah Media

www.molahmedia.com

Printed and Distributed by Ingramspark

ISBN: 978-1-912551-03-3

Dedication

This is for all the entrepreneurs who have the spirit of success, the mentality of investment and the desire to build dreams into the physical. As you go through this book, you should always remember to be exclusively you.

This book is for you if:

- You want to see the results and success you desire in your business

- You want to increase the value of your business

- You are serious about leaving a legacy through building a sustainable business

- Your business is 1-5 years old

- You are ready to step out of your comfort zone and bring value to others.

In this book, you will learn:

- How to build systems and strategies that increase the efficiency of your business

- How to manage your time effectively and invest it more wisely

- How to stay accountable along the course of your business journey

- How to measure the success of the strategies you are using

- How to generate more sales and increase your revenue.

Testimonials and Reviews

'*Master the Basics* by Dean Williams is a solidly grounded book that's useful for any budding entrepreneur or a seasoned leader in business wanting to reinforce some best practices and enhance their learning. It is an enjoyable and intuitive read with many valuable tips, which are reinforced with workbooks and templates to complete. A very effective book for laying down the foundations for a good business or strategy.' **Tunji Akintokun**

'Dean Williams is a once in a lifetime mentor. His unique approach, passion for business and wealth of knowledge is second to none. Since working with Exclusive Visions, my business has expanded considerably. I have gone from a woman who loved helping people publish books to a woman with a business, strategy and plan. Since applying all that I have learnt, I have expanded my team, tested new and innovative ideas, added much more value to my business, implemented and reviewed my business model as well as tripled my income and had a steady stream of customers. Dean's approach is firm but fair and it is so refreshing to work with someone who not only understands your vision but is passionate about helping you to create systems so that you not only have a business but more than that, a legacy. **Master the Basics** is packed full of valuable information, that if implemented, can make a world of difference to your business and those that you serve.' **Daniella Blechner, Founder of Conscious Dreams Publishing and author of *Mr Wrong***

'With anything in life, once you master the basics, you can build on that strong foundation. This book is for entrepreneurs who are serious about mastering the basics of their business model and want to serve their ideal clients. Dean's passion drives him to help novice entrepreneurs reach their desired business goals. When I have worked with other business mentors, I have been left with helpful jigsaw pieces with little understanding of how or why they fit together. Dean Williams and his step-by-step way of working has helped me to really understand how all my business activities are connected. This book is a culmination of the activities, which if done consistently, will help you too with your business goals. Thank you Dean.' **Usha Chudasama, Child and Adult Psychotherapist and author of *Your Happy Child***

'The book provides an excellent road map to any individual seeking to start a business and ultimately accelerate learning and success.' **Rashada Harry, Founder of Your Future, Your Ambition**

'Dean is amazing. I did his **Master the Basics** programme throughout the spring and summer of 2017. During that time, I was at my most productive because he really helped me keep on track and achieve my goals. I have worked with many mentors, but Dean is definitely one of the best out there: punctual, easy to get on with and great at breaking things down. If you're serious about making major changes in your business or feel lost with what to do next, I highly recommend Dean Williams.' **Charlotte Crowl, Cancer Survivor, Founder of Pure Helps to Cure and author of** *Cancer: The Hidden Truth*

'Dean is one of the most inspiring people I have had the pleasure of meeting in 2017. He is on the cusp of becoming a visionary leader and an unwavering motivator. Despite my initial lack of enthusiasm, Dean saw potential in me and offered the guidance I needed to launch my £64,000 crowdfunding campaign, #StratfordToHarvard. I am very humbled to share that it was a complete success with over 700 people donating from the US, UK, Jamaica, Canada and Spain. I have just finished my first semester at Harvard studying Anthropology, Computer Science, African American Studies and Engineering Science. I am excited to see how Dean will continue to inspire generations!' **Isaiah Wellington-Lynn, British student at Harvard University**

'I've been running my catering business for many years — five to be precise. Within that period, I've never understood how the background work of my business operated and the essentials I needed to refine. This meant work was irregular and unstable, feedback was mixed and faults went unnoticed. I've recently started working with Dean Williams. He's opened a portal to a fountain of knowledge, and I now acknowledge the importance of refining certain aspects of the business and having someone to hold me accountable to the business challenges I face. I can also turn to him with any questions about running a business.' **Ruben Ferreira, Cake Specialist and owner of Mr Bakeys**

'The reason I came to Exclusive Visions was because I knew they had lots of invaluable tools that I needed to access and implement to take my business to the next level. Before working on my business, we worked on me — getting rid of the bad habits that I had that were preventing me from getting to that next level and developing new habits that would. We also worked on systemising my business so that it could run without me. Working with Exclusive Visions has not only developed my business but me as an entrepreneur. Invaluable.' **CEO 'Money Mike', Wealth and Business Consultant**

Contents

Acknowledgements

To my top mentor Vonley Joseph — even though you keep denying that you're not my mentor, I appreciate all the mentoring you have given me over the years.

Mr. Consistent, Dengel Robinson — you are the sounding board that I need, and that trusted person who always tells me what I did not want to hear. Your input has allowed me to refine what I know and now I have a diamond of a book. Thank you.

Patrick Bet David — you have inspired me to be the best entrepreneur that I can be. Your videos on Valuetainment are the foundation of my business education. Keep being phenomenal.

Mr. Dependable, Alex Adeosun — you came in and contributed wonderfully to this book. Your writing skills have enhanced the content and I appreciate your dedication and your attitude to producing a chapter of significance and value.

Rhoda, my editor — thank you for helping me refine this rough diamond and turn it into a brilliant masterpiece. Your attention to detail and going beyond the call of duty helped to create this sparkling gem. Rhoda, you are the 'R' in refined. Thank you.

Nadia, my typesetter — I cannot think of anyone better to have designed this book than you. If I was to describe you in one word, it would be 'genius.' You added a touch of class to this book and made it phenomenal.

Finally, the best Book Journey Mentor in the world, Danni Blechner — you supported and helped me to remain focused. I appreciate the proverbial kick up the ass you gave me to stay on task and produce a book of quality that will serve many generations to come.

Foreword

It has been a delight to serve as Dean's mentor over the past five years. I have found him to be a determined and ambitious individual who demonstrates remarkable foresight. These characteristics have enabled him to achieve many goals, one of which is to write this book.

Master the Basics will help new entrepreneurs grasp a basic understanding of what they need to do to progress their business to the next level. Many folk start a business without a firm understanding of the essentials or the practicalities of what makes a business succeed. Dean has been nurturing entrepreneurs for several years now, and he is clearly committed to his clients and their success. They not only benefit from his in-depth knowledge of the business environment but also his enthusiasm. As he supports his clients all along their journey from budding entrepreneur right through to bona fide business owner, he has first-hand knowledge of what it takes to get to the top, what pitfalls to avoid and what works. He has brought all that he has seen and applied into one book, giving anyone who wants to become a competent entrepreneur the tools to do so. In addition, the principles that Dean teaches can also lead to personal growth and development.

This book will test the reader's mindset and really encourage them to do what it takes to become proficient as an entrepreneur. Indeed, anyone who is proactive and keen to learn will benefit from the insights revealed in *Master the Basics*.

Vonley Joseph *provides specialist practical sales training, supporting the development of micro, SME and MNC. He is also an entrepreneur running several businesses in the UK and overseas.*

About Exclusive Visions

'Logic will get you from A to B. Imagination will take you everywhere.' Albert Einstein

=XCLUSIV= VISIONS

Exclusive Visions is a business consultancy, founded by Dean Willliams, that focuses on working with companies that have been in operation for 1-5 years. The most challenging time for a new business is in the first five years. Exclusive Visions works to minimise the trials and errors that most businesses face and helps to create a sustainable model that delivers the entrepreneur's vision. We specialise in refining business models, strategy and systems. In doing so, we help to:

- Create clear goals and objectives
- Generate greater revenue and profit
- Create quality leads and a system to retain them
- Create a functional business structure
- Undertake effective self-assessment
- Create a sustainable business that allows the entrepreneur to stay focused on their vision

Exclusive Visions was founded in 2012 and, as a young company, understands the needs of new business owners. During our own journey, we have been inspired to share our knowledge and have developed a passion to help entrepreneurs create the right business model and strategy that ensures business success.

OUR VISION STATEMENT:

'Creating a vision is what you do, making it a reality is what we do.'

About This Book

Master The Basics brings together the learnings and philosophies of Exclusive Visions. Through extensive research, one of the things we have discovered is that there are eight key principles that a business must follow to create a solid foundation for growth. This book will discuss these key principles which will support you on your entrepreneurial journey.

Exclusive Visions also understands the importance of building the entrepreneur as well as the business. This is achieved through what we call the *Three Nexus of an Entrepreneur.* The *Three Nexus of an Entrepreneur* is a system that incorporates the spiritual, mental and physical development of the individual, which in turn helps to develop a well-rounded business. The strategies and tools within this book will help you build the *Three Nexus of an Entrepreneur.*

As you read this book and implement what you have learnt, I want you to remember three things: *be authentic, be disciplined, be exclusively you.*

Getting Started

'Success is neither magical nor mysterious.
Success is the natural consequence of consistently
applying the basic fundamentals.' **Jim Rohn**

You will need:

- A pen

- Notebook

- Access to the internet

- A 'can do, will do' attitude

I, Dean Williams, will be your guide throughout this book,

'When you believe it, you will see it and achieve it.
Awooo!'

Bruce Lee said 'I fear not the man who has practiced 10,000 kicks once, but I fear the man who has practiced one kick 10,000 times.' From this, we can infer that a fundamental principle of growth and success is becoming a master at your chosen skill. No matter how simple or complex, to master that *one* thing you must start with the basics.

Often we are easily excited by the grand things, not realising that the glamour and sparkle of a truly successful business is the result of a consistent effort to acquire and master fundamental principles that sustain growth and development. The process is tedious which is why we often ignore it. In addition, we also have a tendency to focus on short term superficial success, forgetting that creating a business that leaves a legacy should be part of the long-term vision. We get side-tracked by creating a glitzy and expensive website, advertising, office space, uniforms, etc.

Though these are important, they are not key to creating your foundation. What does foundation mean? In relation to business, a foundation refers to a system that allows your company to generate increasing revenue, replicate the same success when those principles are applied to a new business venture and create quality time for both you and your loved ones.

The Cycle of Entrepreneurial Mastery

'Success isn't always about greatness. It's about consistency. Consistent hard work leads to success. Greatness will come.'
Dwayne Johnson

Form vs formless

At the beginning of any learning journey, you need a structure, plan, curriculum or form to enable you to acquire basic knowledge. This is then followed by practical and technical learning that allows you to gain competence. Formlessness is transcending and mastering a skill so that you become unconsciously competent at that skill. Consistency, effort, discipline and commitment are essential for this transformation. As you journey to mastery, you go through three phases as shown in Figure i:

1. Formless: Tyro

2. Form: Competent

3. Formless: Mastery

Formless (tyro)

Learning a new skill can be daunting and confusing but in the midst of it all is a wonderful challenge to grow and learn. Do you remember learning to ride your bike? It seemed impossible, but stabilisers helped you to balance, allowing you to build up your confidence. Starting a business is much the same as learning to ride a bike. In the beginning, you do all that you can help build your confidence. You might:

- Take a short course
- Read recommended books
- Go to seminars
- Find a mentor
- Watch videos
- Complete a business plan (don't get me started on this one!)

As you start any new undertaking, you have no system or form. You are a formless tyro and you need to equip yourself with the tools, knowledge and resources to achieve success. What this means is that you must take inventory of what you know and what you need to learn. This is the first step in creating your foundation.

'Confidence comes from being competent in what you do.'

Form (competent)

Let's say, at this stage, you have run your business for anywhere between 1-3 years. The stabilisers are off and you are seeing results. Your strategy is taking shape. You took your time to understand the rules of engagement of the entrepreneurial world. You did not rush or spend your money on intricate and flashy items like many entrepreneurs do, as you know that having flashy items does not make you an excellent entrepreneur. You invested in mastering the basics and creating systems within your business. As a result, you are now competent at running your business and familiar with the systems you have created to keep your business running.

At this point, I have the urge to share an insightful story with you:

A man wanted to be the best chef in the world because he saw the life of a master chef as an exciting adventure. So, he set out by first talking to as many master chefs as possible to understand how to get to the top. There were two chefs in particular that influenced and inspired him. He went to the first chef who was a master cake maker and asked him what he did to master his field.

The chef simply replied, 'I learnt how to make the best basic sponge cake.'

Disappointed with the response, the man went to another chef and asked the same question.

'What did you do to become a master chef?'

The second chef who was renowned for making exquisite sauces replied, 'I made the basic sauce over 5000 times.'

Again, the man was disappointed with the response. Maybe these guys didn't know about all the wonderful automated gadgets out there that could make fancy stuff. So, he rented a shop and bought top-of-the-range equipment to create his recipes. He was excited but after a while became disheartened as nothing he made tasted good.

He met both the chefs again and asked them why he could not create tasty dishes.

'I have the best equipment and the best ingredients but I can't create a simple, successful recipe.'

The first chef replied, 'I can make all kinds of cakes because I learnt to master the basic sponge cake, and because of that I can create over 1000 different cakes.'

The second chef replied, 'The reason why people love my unique sauces is because I mastered the basic sauces and this gave me the confidence to vary the mixture by adding new ingredients to create new flavours.'

Understanding his folly, the man sold all his equipment, gave away his ingredients and went back to the chefs and said, 'Please teach me the basics.'

'Save yourself time, energy and money now by mastering the basics.'

Most of your effort will be needed in the early stages of your development, but as you grow and refine your skills and knowledge, you will see that what was once challenging is now an unconscious competent act. To be truly confident in your chosen skill, you must become competent and that only happens when you have mastered the basics.

Formless (mastery)

What does it mean to be a master? Is it that you are more skilled or more knowledgeable than others?

Mastery is the end product of dedication to the refinement and innovation of a chosen endeavour. Bruce Lee is a perfect example of someone who achieved a level of mastery. His dedication was exemplary. What he did in the world of martial arts was to take what he liked, discard what he didn't like and add what was uniquely his and create a new form of martial arts called Jeet Kune Do. This is exactly what you will need to do. Master your chosen skill and be the authority figure in your chosen field. Through growth, refinement and innovation, you will be able to capture the value perceived by your target audience. Satisfied customers are advocates for your business, and this is a sure testament of one having achieved mastery.

'To become a master at any skill, it takes the total effort of your heart, mind, and soul working together in tandem.'
Maurice Young

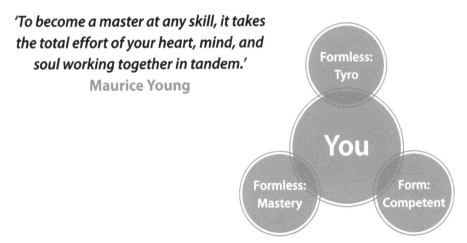

Figure i: The cycle of entrepreneurial mastery

I urge all my clients to master their chosen skill before embarking on a new frontier.

Love what you do

Love what you do as love is the foundation of all things. The LOVE® used by Exclusive Visions, is a great illustration of this. It stands for:

Leadership: Before you can lead others, you need to be able to lead yourself. Master yourself spiritually, mentally and physically and you will find it easier to lead others.

Organisation: You cannot create anything great if they are not organised; ensure your thoughts are well structured.

Vision: You do not need to know how the vision will manifest because the how is not as important as the *why*. Make sure you create a compelling *why* that draws upon the imagination of your target audience.

Empowerment: The people who believe in your *why* are there to support their dream while building yours. Equip them with the skills and knowledge needed so that they don't feel discouraged when times get hard. If they are well prepared, they will not only build their vision but help to build yours.

To be a master you must:

- Dedicate yourself
- Learn
- Innovate
- Teach others
- Know who you are
- Be flexible

Time dedicated to mastering the basics is the cornerstone to long lasting success.

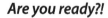

Are you ready?!

Setting Goals Using the SHIE Matrix

*'Loss provides an opportunity to take inventory of our lives,
to reconsider priorities, and to determine new directions.'*
Gerald Lawson Sittser

As an entrepreneur, it's important to remain balanced. To do this, we must take inventory of ourselves. We become so focused on managing the business, clients and employees that we forget ourselves. These areas are important, but we should not overlook the importance of refining and developing ourselves along the journey. *The Strength, Habits, Implementation and Education (SHIE) Matrix* illustrates the key areas you need to reflect on and refine to grow and develop you and your business. These areas are critical to your progress and will ensure that you can handle any unforeseen challenges that you will inevitably face along your business journey. The SHIE Matrix does require that you are honest with yourself and prepared to change your mindset and habits. More about this later.

First, let's talk a bit more about *The Three Nexus of an Entrepreneur.*

The Three Nexus of an Entrepreneur

When building a business, many people tend to forget the most important factor within it: themselves. You are the blueprint of what your business will ultimately become. Therefore, it is imperative that you continue to refine yourself as an individual, consistently, on all levels: mentally, spiritually and physically. These are *The Three Nexus of an Entrepreneur.*

Why? First of all, your business is an extension of you. It represents your inherent values and desires for your customers. In business, no one is an island. You have to work with others, therefore, communication skills are key not just in relation to building relationships with your customers but with other stakeholders that can assist or leverage your business. It is important to refine who you are as an individual so that you are better able to enter the world of business adept at dealing with others thus tapping into your market. Tapping into your market will, in turn, allow others to tap into your products and services thus increasing profitability, sustainability and customer experience. To be able to do this, developing your emotional intelligence, listening skills, communication skills, as well learning new things is key. It's how we tackle difficult situations that make or break us. Running a business can also be physically tiring so it is important to ensure that we are physically fit. This is why at Exclusive Visions, we start with developing the *Three Nexus of an Entrepreneur.*

What are the Nexus?

Spirituality: We help the individual develop the intangible qualities, attributes and skills needed to be a successful entrepreneur. These include self-motivation, passion, purpose, your why, persistence and patience.

Mentality: Mental development looks not only at the acquisition of knowledge but also its application, tactical planning and strategising needed to utilise this knowledge. It includes taking inventory of self, integrity and character, creating a monomaniacal focus and surrounding yourself with progressive industry leaders.

Physicality: You need to be physically fit to endure the journey. With the support of our key partners, Exclusive Visions helps clients develop the right eating habits, an effective exercise routine and incorporate meditation, rest and having fun. We also help clients develop their brand.

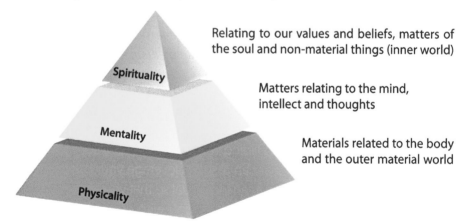

Relating to our values and beliefs, matters of the soul and non-material things (inner world)

Matters relating to the mind, intellect and thoughts

Materials related to the body and the outer material world

Spirituality

Mentality

Physicality

Figure ii: The Three Nexus of an Entrepreneur

Setting New Standards to Achieve Your Goals

How many goals have you set over the last 12 months? How many of these have you achieved? How many times did you swear to yourself that *'this time, this time, I will actually make it happen?'* There is a saying 'The level of thinking that got you to where you are now is not designed to get you to where you want to be.' Ask yourself these questions:

- What habits do I need to refine or get rid of?
- Who do I need to collaborate with and who can guide me?
- What knowledge and skillset do I need to become the authority in my field?

By answering these fundamental questions and implementing the answers, you will be well on your way to achieving any goals that you set.

Author of *The 10-Second Philosophy*, Derek Mills, otherwise known as 'The Standards Guy' says 'A standard is a rule, a quality, basis, level, or criterion you live by each day, which honours and is congruent with the real you inside.' The standards you set today will ultimately achieve your goals for tomorrow. Ask yourself what standards you are setting daily and how you can raise them so that they are in alignment with your vision?

Taking Inventory Using the SHIE Matrix

Before you set a goal, it's important to look closely at your core values. The SHIE Matrix (shown in Figure iii) enables you to identify your core elements that align you to your goal or vision.

There are four components to the SHIE Matrix: Strengths, Habits, Implementation, Education. By taking inventory and using the SHIE Matrix, you are able to identify and develop key strengths, recognise disruptive habits as well as implement new behaviours and educational routes to gain the knowledge needed to refine yourself and your business.

All four elements of the Matrix are both qualitative and quantitative. The qualitative component means that you can identify shortfalls and refine these. The quantitative component is essential as this measures attainment level and gives you a discrete measurement of achievement.

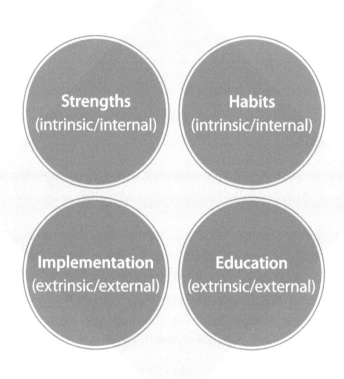

Figure iii: The SHIE Matrix

KEY TERMS

Qualitative: relating to, measuring, or measured by the quality of something rather than its quantity, e.g., how well your book was written.

Quantitative: relating to, measuring, or measured by the quantity of something rather than its quality, e.g., time, weight etc.

The four components of the SHIE Matrix

Strengths: By focusing and developing your attributes as an individual and entrepreneur, you will generate results for your business. You will increase your efficiency and obtain consistent results.

> **Example:** *Your three strengths are sales, people development and networking, while your weaknesses are administration, IT and systems set-up. It's important to understand your weaknesses but, by developing your strengths, you will create opportunities to improve those weaknesses. By developing your skills in sales, you will be able to increase your revenue which in turn will allow you to hire two new employees who can manage your admin and IT. How do you know they will fit into your company? Your good networking skills mean that you can identify and connect with quality individuals. Your ability to develop people means you provide top class training programmes. Therefore, by using your strengths, you have managed your weaknesses.*

What are your three key strengths?	How will you augment them?	How will this build you and your business?

Habits: The Collins[1] dictionary defines a habit as 'something you do often or regularly.' I like to define a habit as, 'an action performed consistently over time that makes an individual unconsciously competent at the chosen activity.' We know that habits can be good and bad, so it's imperative that you replace bad habits with those that contribute to success.

---

1   www.collinsdictionary.com/dictionary/english/habit

Example: A habit common to all of us, including entrepreneurs, is procrastination. Starting something and not finishing it (like that book you said you'll write), putting things off until tomorrow and completing everything on your to-do list, except the most important task are all examples of procrastination. Procrastination impedes progress.

However, any bad habit can be replaced by a good habit. Nature doesn't like vacuums, so if you take something away, it must be replaced. Procrastination can be replaced with…*action*. All you need is focus. When you know you need to get something done, get it done. Later in the book, you will see how you can ensure that you implement new habits.

Complete the exercises below. Which habits can be replaced with more effective ones and how will this benefit your business?

What habit do you need to replace?	Which habit will replace this?	How will this build you and your business?

Implementation: You are motivated and excited as you can see success on the horizon. Before you go any further, let me manage your expectations as I don't want you to overdose on the drug called 'hopium' (the love of hoping and not doing). Identifying your strengths is one thing, but if you don't use them, you won't develop those new habits and success will remain out of reach, stuck on that horizon. To get to success, there are three things you must invest.

- Time
- Effort
- Money

The first thing you should do is set new standards. Before you read any further, please watch the two videos about standards from my mentors Derek Mills and Patrick Bet David.

Derek Mills:	Patrick Bet David:
www.youtube.com/ watch?v=Ca0G1qJOlng	www.youtube.com/ watch?v=hpTfQA6HIpY&t=49s

What three things will you implement to create the right habits and develop your strengths?	How will you do this?	How will this build you and your business?
Set new standards		

Education: Benjamin Franklin said this about education 'An investment in knowledge pays the best interest.' The word *educate* derives from the Latin word *educat*, meaning 'led out', and from the verb *educare*, related to *educere* meaning 'lead out.' What we can establish from the Latin derivation is that:

1. Education is not only the acquisition of data and knowledge.

2. Education, to be authentic, must also come *out* of the individual by refining their thinking, skills and abilities using their own efforts. A good education gives you the tools to not only receive but also seek out knowledge.

If you want to be taken seriously in your chosen field, you must be an avid reader and actively seek new experiences. You must socialise, grow and innovate. You can't imitate others and regurgitate their words. You must be authentic and set a precedence. This is how your customers will buy into your product and services.

You must learn about your customers' needs and wants, new technologies in your market and your competitors' strategies. Understanding past events, awareness of the present and anticipating what's coming will go a long way to making you an expert in your field.

What do you need to learn?	How will you do it?	How will this build you and your business?

Without further ado, let's start the process of setting your goals.
Yay!

Exclusive Visions' Goal Roadmap

Choosing your goal

So you've taken inventory using the SHIE Matrix, and now it's time to set those goals! First, it's imperative to remember that your ultimate goal, e.g., creating a billion-pound business, is met by achieving a series of objectives leading up to that ultimate prize. Getting to billionaire status will start with, for example, increasing each year's profits by 10%. Define the objectives you need to meet to get to your final destination.

What are objectives?

Objectives are the stepping stones towards achieving your goals. They are:

- Specific actions or efforts that support the attainment of your goals
- Tangible
- Quantifiable

The Goal Roadmap, shown in Figure iv, will help you set achievable goals for both your business and personal life. It allows you to visualise where you are on your journey and keep you on track until you have reached your goal.

HOW TO USE YOUR GOAL ROADMAP

★ **Define your goal**

Find an image that represents your goal and place it in the box indicated on the map

★ **Is your goal short-term or medium-term? Define a timescale within which to achieve this goal**

Short-term goals are usually achieved within 12 months
Medium-term goals are usually achieved within 12 – 18 months

★ **Define your objective**

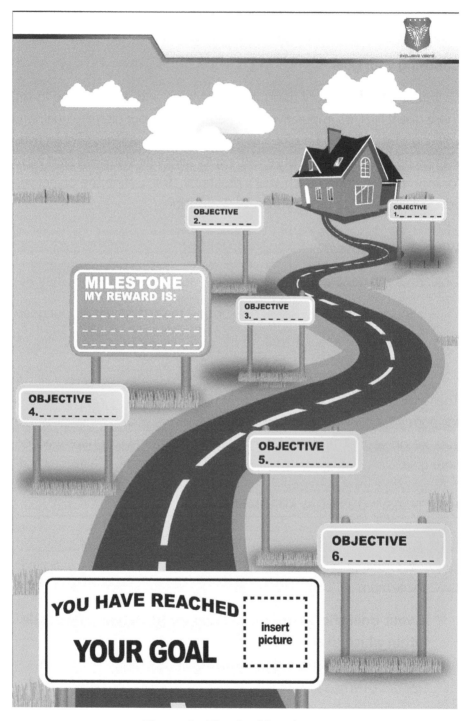

Figure iv: The Goal Roadmap

Define your objectives in clusters, e.g., the first three, then the next three, etc.

My objectives:

① _____

② _____

③ _____

Select images that represent your objectives and place on your goal roadmap.

★ Milestone Reward ★

Your journey is about you, so the halfway point is a testament to your efforts. Once you make it to the halfway mark, you might hit a plateau. Rather than get discouraged, look at what you've achieved so far and take a moment to reflect and appreciate the work you have accomplished. Acknowledge that you are halfway to your goal.

Keep the momentum by looking back at your progress and replicating the activities that have been fruitful you and discarding the activities that haven't.

You have got to reward for yourself once you complete the first three objectives. Celebrating the milestone markers will help you stay motivated.

My milestone reward is:

_____

_____

_____

The last three objectives

These last three objectives are the only things standing between you and your goal. With the first three, you should have gained knowledge and acquired new skills that can help you refine your last three objectives.

Ensure that you take the time to review your objectives. Achieving these last three depend on this review. Remember, the goal is always the same but the objectives you choose must remain flexible as things will change along the way.

I always say to my clients:

'On the road towards your goals, you need to be as flexible as a young bamboo tree.'

Revised objectives:

4 _____

5 _____

6 _____

Achieving your objectives to get your goal

You can see that achieving your goals means implementing the components of the SHIE Matrix. This, in turn, requires three behavioural traits which I fondly refer to as DCC. They are:

- Discipline
- Commitment
- Consistency

Discipline: staying focused on attaining an individual's dreams through continual improvement and refinement of one's habits, knowledge and skills.

Commitment: continual dedication to a decision made long after the emotion and excitement have worn off.

Consistency: continuous practice to maintain and improve standards over a period of time in order to achieve desired results.

Whilst setting the objectives may seem easy, staying disciplined, committed and consistent can be challenging. In order to see the success you desire, one must beat the infamous enemy called procrastination and instil DCC... and to apply these traits faithfully, you will need to replace procrastination with action!

⑧ Principles of Mastering the Basics

Part 1:
Creating the System

'Organise around business functions, not people.
Build systems within each business function.
Let systems run the business and people run the systems.
People come and go but the systems remain constant.'
Michael Gerber, *E-Myth Revisited*

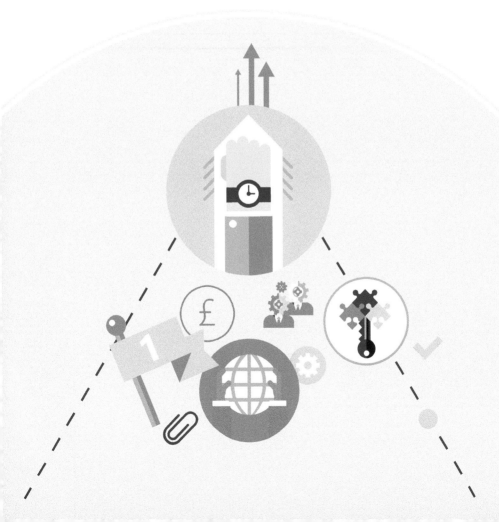

Principle #1: Create the Right Business Strategy

'Perception is strong and sight weak.
In strategy it is important to see distant things
as if they were close and to take a distanced view of close things.'
Miyamoto Musashi, legendary Japanese swordsman

What is Strategy?

Strategy is defined as 'a plan of action designed to achieve a long-term or overall aim.' It's derived from the Greek word, *strategos*, meaning 'the art of the general' or the 'art for arrangement' of troops. One of the greatest strategists to have ever lived, Sun Tzu, author of *The Art of War* said that war, 'is a matter of life and death. A road either to safety or ruin.'

A strategy is the engine of your business model. It will drive your plan and vision. Trying to run a business without one is like having a Ferrari with no engine. It may look good, but it will go straight to nowhere. Imagine the destination as the vision, the Ferrari as the plan and the engine as the strategy. Without the driving force of the engine, the vision can never be met.

KEY TERMS

Vision: this is your 'why' or the heartbeat of the business that anchors and motivates you and your team.

Plan: this defines what needs to be done to achieve your why, your vision and your mission.

Strategy: this defines how the plan will proceed in order to obtain the vision.

The Seven Steps to Building an Effective Strategy

There are many tools and resources that will help you create and implement the right strategy for you. YouTube, Udemy and your local library will provide a plethora of information. However, keeping to our principle of mastering the basics, here are my seven steps to help you acquire the mindset of a strategist.

1 Know thyself: who are you and what do you do?

As Socrates once said 'to know thyself is the beginning of wisdom.' If you don't know who you are, what you do and what you offer, then how can you expect anyone else to? It is imperative to know the identity of your business — this is your *'why.'*

Your identity is the key to creating a great Value Proposition for your customers. Your key Value Proposition is a statement that perfectly summarises what your business is and the products and services you offer. A great Value Proposition is one that allows your potential customer to buy into your product or service. We will expand on Value Propositions more when we discuss Principle #4 of Master the Basics.

For example, Airbnb's Value Proposition is that it provides a service for travellers, helping them to find alternative accommodation to hotels that closely suits their requirements at a reasonable price. It also provides an extra income to those renting their space as holiday accommodation.

What is your business Value Proposition?

_____

_____

2 Determine your purpose and core values

The purpose of your business is its role and function. Why does it exist? What value and significance does it bring to the market?

Core values are integral to any business as they underpin the purpose of the business. They uphold both the purpose and vision. They are the guiding principles that should not be compromised on as this will compromise the business. The core values are what should drive every decision and subsequent action.

My suggestion is to establish a maximum of ten core values that are essential to your business. These core values should represent your purpose, mission, ethos and brand. Table 1.1 below lists some values that you can choose from, or you can create your own. Jot down an explanation as to how this value is demonstrated in your business. Appendix 3 on page 133 lists the core values for Exclusive Visions and can help you define the value of each for your company.

Table 1.1: Core values

Acceptance	Accessibility	Accomplishment	Adaptability	Affection	Appreciation
Approachability	Assertiveness	Assurance	Attentiveness	Awareness	Balance
Belonging	Bliss	Bravery	Calm	Care	Cheerfulness
Clarity	Closeness	Commitment	Community	Compassion	Competence
Completion	Composure	Confidence	Connection	Consistency	Contentment
Contribution	Conviction	Cooperation	Courage	Courtesy	Creativity
Credibility	Curiosity	Dependability	Depth	Desire	Determination
Diligence	Discipline	Drive	Duty	Effectiveness	Efficiency
Empathy	Encouragement	Endurance	Energy	Enjoyment	Enthusiasm
Excellence	Excitement	Expressiveness	Exuberance	Fairness	Faith
Family	Fearlessness	Fierceness	Fitness	Flexibility	Fluency
Focus	Fortitude	Freedom	Friendliness	Friendship	Fun
Generosity	Giving	Grace	Gratitude	Growth	Guidance
Happiness	Harmony	Health	Helpfulness	Honesty	Honour
Hopefulness	Humour	Imagination	Independence	Individuality	Inquisitiveness
Inspiration	Integrity	Intelligence	Intimacy	Introspection	Intuition
Involvement	Joy	Kindness	Learning	Liveliness	Longevity
Love	Loyalty	Maturity	Meaning	Mindfulness	Motivation
Open-minded	Openness	Optimism	Organisation	Patience	Peace
Perceptiveness	Perseverance	Persistence	Playfulness	Pleasure	Presence
Reasonableness	Reflection	Relaxation	Reliability	Resilience	Respect
Responsibility	Restraint	Reverence	Satisfaction	Security	Self-control
Selflessness	Self-reliance	Sexuality	Simplicity	Sincerity	Skilfulness
Spirituality	Stability	Strength	Success	Support	Teamwork
Thankfulness	Thoroughness	Thoughtfulness	Trust	Truth	Understanding
Usefulness	Virtue	Willingness	Wisdom	Wonder	Youthfulness

My top ten core values

1 _____

2 _____

3 _____

4 _____

5 _____

6 _____

7 _____

8 _____

9 _____

10 _____

③ Define the challenges that you are solving for your customers

Your business should provide solutions. To do so, you need to know what difficulties your business will solve. You should be able to define this in a short statement.

Airbnb solves the problem of endless searches for hotels that are often over-priced, not available when you need them, and not guaranteed to be within distance of the 'hot-spots.' During high season, or popular conventions or events, Airbnb provides a more homely and affordable alternative to hotels.

Think about your business. Have you identified a gap within your market? Are you filling that gap in a way that's not only useful but also original?

What challenges you are solving for your customer?

_____

_____

_____

④ Select the right KPIs & KVIs

Your strategies and plans need to be measured to test their effectiveness and validity. Your method of measuring needs to make sense to your business.

A Key Performance Indicator (KPI) is 'a quantifiable measure used to evaluate the success of an organisation, employee, etc. in meeting objectives for performance.' We will go into further detail later on in the book.

KPIs and critical numbers should measure up to the integrity of your business (brand promises). Your brand promise should mirror your purpose and core values. This acts as the spine of your business.

By using quantitative metrics, you can measure the success of both individuals and teams. You can easily track when an individual or team is achieving or exceeding their goals. Success must be rewarded, and these rewards should be in alignment with your brand. KPIs also allow you to track where individuals or teams may be underperforming, and it is up to you, as the business owner, to make decisions about whether it is the strategies used that need refining or the individual/team.

It's important to note that we will be discussing KPIs as well as Key Value Indicators (KVIs) as this will give you a greater overall insight into your business. More on this subject later.

⑤ Assign the right roles and keep your team accountable

Key metrics can be achieved by delegating the right task to the best individuals within the team. It's important that everybody within the business has a clear and identifiable role and sound understanding of their responsibilities. As a manager, clear expectations of each role should be set and actionable items assigned to specific people. Each member of the team should be clear about who is doing what within the team to enable efficiency and consistency.

Make a list of each member of your team and their roles and responsibilities below, even if that's just you!

Name	Role	Responsibilities	Are these responsibilities appropriate? Y/N How/Why not?	What responsibilities would be more suitable?

⑥ Know your market: who and where is your customer?

Do you know who your ideal customer is? Have you created a customer profile? A customer profile should contain all the information you need to know about them. You need to be familiar with their habits, likes, dislikes, pain points and find out where they 'hang out.' It is important to have a good sense of who your target customers are. You may want to think about the size of your market segments at this stage to ensure you have enough potential customers to build a sustainable business.

Airbnb's target audience are those who want to travel abroad, may have a limited income and want somewhere affordable but comfortable to stay. They can be independent travellers, couples or families.

Use the exercise below to create your own customer profile. Draw an image of your customer. Give your customer a name. Label your customer with some of the following and create some of your own:

- Gender
- Background/culture/religion
- Beliefs
- Job role
- Marital status
- Sexuality
- Interests
- Dislikes
- Current challenges
- Magazines/newspapers they read
- Salary
- Online and offline hangouts
- Their network

Think about your most valued clients so far. What were their most pressing needs and how did you solve them? A good practice is to offer each client a feedback form or short survey after delivering your service, so you can assess performance. It is this that will best help you understand your customers' needs. It will also help you create a more authentic customer profile.

Customer name _____

7 Know your competition — they are not your enemy

Competitors will always exist. You just need to define what makes your business the best, unique or worth your customers money. Beating your competitor is not about offering lower rates. It's about adding extra value, creating an experience and being authentic, so that the customers in your market will single you out. One thing to note is that your competitor is not your enemy. They are businesses that offer similar products or services to your market. In spite of this, they can and will assist you on your journey if you choose to.

I will urge you to examine the competitors that complement your core values and see if there is any synergy that will help you work in partnership. If it works for Apple, Samsung and HTC, then it can work for you!

List your main competitors and write down how you could potentially work with them or what you could learn from them.

Competitor	How can I work with them?	What can I learn from them?

What happens next?

Now that you've learnt about the components to build your strategy, it's imperative that you test the hypothesis. You must test the model before you invest any more money into your business. Finding out which components work and which do not, will help you to refine your business and help create an effective system that will free up your time and energy. This will minimise the trials and errors that entrepreneurs come up against and ensure that you have a greater chance of success.

To figure out if you're on the right track with your business strategy, I highly suggest you find ways of interacting with and learning from your target market. Find out if they really have the problem that you think they have and if your product or service is the solution.

You can do this in a number of ways:

- **Speaking events**

    This is an excellent opportunity to interact with your potential clients face to face and gain a greater understanding of who they are and what they need. I suggest that you research what events, meet ups, conferences and seminars are scheduled throughout the calendar year cover topics within your field. Contact the events manager and put yourself forward to speak at their event. Additionally, you can host your own events. It's also a good idea to partner with other experts or organisations who serve your target market. This will help attendance.

- **Questionnaires / surveys**

    Using questionnaires or tools such as surveymonkey[2] or typeform[3] allows you to collect all the necessary information that will help you understand the needs of your potential clients. By posing specific and targeted questions, you will be able to identify what is working well within your business as well as your customers' pain points. This will help you to refine your services and enable you to know exactly how you can offer more value.

- **Feedback forms**

    Whilst you may feel that you have provided an excellent service, your customers may feel otherwise. It is therefore imperative that you do not act on your own assumptions but take the time to check in with your clients to find out if you have met or exceeded their needs as well as where and how you may need to improve your service or product.

---

2 www.surveymonkey.com
3 www.typeform.com

Principle #2: Build Your Business Model

'Burger King's business model was broken. But it was like sex in the '50s. Everyone knew it, but no one would talk about it.'
Greg Brenneman

A business model is a plan or blueprint for the successful operation of a business which includes sources of revenue, products and services, customer base and financing. The plan includes what products and services will be created and how they will be brought to market. Its aim is to identify exactly how the business runs and operates. The aim of the business model is to not only create a blueprint but to help the entrepreneur see exactly what's working effectively and what needs changing. At Exclusive Visions, we prefer to use the alternative to the original business plan, the Business Model Canvas (BMC).

The BMC, originally proposed by Dr Alexander Osterwalder[4], is a great visual tool that allows you to map out, track, describe and challenge the building blocks of your business (Figure 2.1). It's a one-page overview of the key components of your business that clearly defines what you do, how you do it, who you help, how you will reach them and the costs. Alternatively, it can be defined as a strategic management template that highlights elements describing a business' Value Proposition, infrastructure, customers and finances.

It is a great alternative to the usual business plan (at Exclusive Visions, we prefer to use tools that innovate on existing tools) as it allows you to visualise where you are with your business. With this one page, you and your team can jointly map out the different elements needed and refine them as you progress. You can really get creative with a large print-out of your BMC using post-it notes and board markers to map your journey. It enables you to adopt a more hands-on approach that fosters clarity, fruitful discussions, creativity, analysis and problem-solving.

---

4   www.alexosterwalder.com

The BMC is really a living, working document that you will end up referring to regularly as opposed to it being shelved to gather dust in the way business plans are! Let's be honest, business plans are seldom updated

Figure 2.1: Business Model Canvas (BMC)

and referred to once completed. The BMC will overcome this and, as you can see from the figure, it helps the creator and potential investor envisage the model from a bird's eye view.

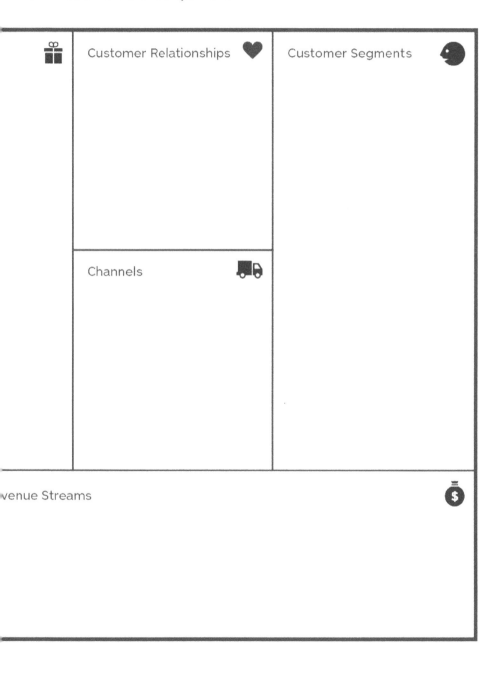

COMPANIES THAT HAVE USED A BMC

- Mastercard
- Xerox
- Fujitsu
- NASA
- PWC
- Intel
- Deloitte
- Oracle
- NatWest
- Virgin

THE FOUR MAIN AREAS OF THE BMC

- Offering
- Customers
- Infrastructure
- Finances

Offering

Value Proposition

A Value Proposition is an innovation, service or feature intended to make a business or product attractive to customers[5], According to Osterwalder (2004), a business' Value Proposition is what differentiates it from its competitors.

To define your Value Proposition, you need to answer these questions:

- What value do you bring to the customer?
- Which one of your customer's problems do you want to solve?
- What bundles of products and services are you offering to each customer segment?
- Which customer needs are you meeting?

The elements of your Value Proposition should be congruent with your vision, core values and your why, and include:

1. **Novelty**: Have a fresh approach to your target market's needs.
2. **Performance**: Your products and services should be easy to use, of a higher quality than competitors and more efficient.

---

5 Oxford Living Dictionary

③ **Customisation**: Ensure that your products and services have been modified to meet the needs of your target market.

④ **'Getting the job done'**: Your product or service helps to complete a task in an efficient and effective way.

⑤ **Design**: Ensure that your product and services stand out and that the design catches your market's attention.

⑥ **Brand/Status**: Create a brand that your customers would be proud to advocate.

⑦ **Price**: The price of your products and services should be in line with what your customer segment sees and is willing to pay for.

⑧ **Cost Reduction**: Think about how you can create a premium product at a competitive price so that you can create more value for you customer.

⑨ **Risk Reduction**: Ensure that your products and services bring peace of mind to your customers by implementing risk reduction strategies such as money back guarantees, warranties and insurance and free trails basis.

⑩ **Accessibility**: Ensure that your products and services are easily available to a wide range of consumers on multiple platforms.

A VALUE PROPOSITION MAY BE:

Quantitative: based on price and efficiency

Qualitative: based on overall customer experience and outcome

The bedrock of a great Value Proposition is to ensure you provide a great service then move on to create a wonderful experience for your clients. Look at the market and submerge yourself in a niche that best fits your product or service. This is where you will operate from and serve your customers.

Customers

Customer segments

- Who are you creating value for?
- Who are your most important customers?

Identifying the customers you wish to serve is paramount. Every successful and effective business knows this. Customers can then be segmented based on common needs, attributes and behaviours. Once your segments are defined, you can carefully design your business model and tailor it to their specific requirements.

Some customer segments:

1. **Mass market**: This market is not segmented. It accounts for the masses who share broadly similar needs and problems. A perfect example of something a mass market may need is a car.

2. **Niche market**: A well-defined, specific market. An example of a product for a niche market would be a Rolex.

3. **Segmented**: A business may further drill down the target market that it has already identified to further distinguish its clients based on gender, age and/or income.

4. **Diverse**: This is a business that serves two customer segments with different needs, problems and characteristics. An example is supermarkets. They have consumers who buy their products, while they themselves are consumers who buy from suppliers.

5. **Multi-sided platform / market**: Some companies will serve multiple interdependent customer segments. For example, Ebay has to cater for consumers needs as well as those of vendors.

This is not an exhaustive list of customer segments but it gives you a foundation from which you can explore and define your market. This then allows you to determine the best way to interact with your chosen market. The way in which you communicate your message your market is essential for building your tribe, so you will need to determine the most effective and efficient way to do this.

Customer relationships

The kind of customer relationships you build are crucial to creating a brand for your business. Knowing what kind of relationships you need to build with them will also help to establish and uniquely identify how you, as a business, interact with your customers.

Here are some questions to answer first:

- What type of relationship does each of our customer segments expect you to have with them?

- Which ones have you established?

- How are they integrated within the rest of your business model?

- What is the cost?

Here are some examples of how to build customer relationships:

1. **Personal assistance**: This is based on human interaction, either face-to-face, via email or over the phone.

2. **Dedicated personal assistance**: This is where a specific representative or member of staff is dedicated to an individual or group of customers. This allows your customer to have a more intimate experience.

3. **Self-service**: This service allows for a level of independence for the customer. There is no direct relationship but the business provides all the tools needed by the customer to help themselves.

④ Automated services: This is a similar system to self-service but offers a more customised service through its automated systems. Automated systems are able to identify individual customers through their individual needs, characteristics and previous buys. For example, Amazon is able to make book suggestions based on the previous books purchased.

⑤ Communities: Many organisations create a community platform that allows direct interaction between multiple clients and the business. This platform provides a space where knowledge can be shared.

⑥ Co-creation: This is where customers can interact with each other as well as a product or service. For example, Amazon enables buyers to write and leave reviews thus providing value and recommendations to other potential buyers.

To really get ahead of the competition, stop thinking about just providing a *service* and start thinking about giving an *experience*. Providing a great service is essential, but it's just the start of building a long-lasting relationship with your customer. Creating *an experience* will give you a competitive advantage as this will create advocates for your business.

Channels

A channel in this context refers to the method you used to deliver your products and services to your target customers. It's important to establish the right combination of channels that will effectively bring your Value Proposition to market. These methods must be fast, efficient and cost effective.

Here are some questions to consider when defining your customer channels:

- How do your customer segments want to be reached?
- How are you currently communicating with them?

- How are your channels integrated?
- Which ones work best?
- Which ones are cost-efficient?
- How are you integrating with your customers' routine?

KEY TERMS

Self-defined / Sole channels, e.g., store-front

Partnered / Joint, e.g., working with major distributors

You can also combine both channels.

The phases of a Value Proposition channel[6]:

1 **Awareness**: how to raise awareness about a business' products and services.

2 **Evaluation**: how to help customers evaluate an organisation's Value Proposition.

3 **Purchase**: how to allow customers to purchase specific products and services.

4 **Delivery**: how to deliver a Value Proposition to customers.

5 **After sales**: how to provide post-purchase customer support.

The channel is not just about supply and demand. It's about the life cycle of the growth and innovation of your product and service. It encompasses how you make your market aware of what you offer, gathering feedback, and using that feedback to innovate your Value Proposition and customer experience. It's vital to always keep the needs of your customer at the forefront of your business decisions. This is a vital component in remaining significant to your customer.

---

6 Pigneur (2010) Business Model Generation. John Wiley and Sons Ltd

Infrastructure

Key activities

The key activities are the most important tasks that need to be carried out for the Value Proposition to reach its target audience. Remember to prioritise the most important task first and get that completed before you move on to secondary ones.

Some considerations:

- What key activities does your Value Proposition require?
- What are your distribution channels?
- What are customer relationships?
- What are your revenue streams?

Categories of key activities:

1 **Production**

2 **Problem solving**

3 **Platform / Network**

If you start with the most important task first, you place your business in a position to build momentum. It's imperative that the activities added to the BMC are aligned to the goal and that way you will stay on track.

Key resources for your Value Proposition

These tools will help you deliver your Value Proposition to your market. These are the most important assets that enable the business model to function effectively. However, they are often overlooked by businesses in the early years. The focus is usually on income (finances), but this is only one of four important resources shown below.

Questions to consider:

- What resources does your Value Proposition need?

- What are your distribution channels?
- What are your revenue streams?

Types of resources:

1. **Physical** (machinery, materials, IT equipment)
2. **Intellectual** (brand, patents, copyright, data)
3. **Human** (customer experience, sales, marketing reps)
4. **Financial** (cash, line of credit, stock options)

Partnerships

You should consider working with a network of suppliers, set up Joint Ventures (JV) or strategic alliances, or partner with sponsors to gain the necessary resources to deliver your Value Proposition.

Questions about partnerships:

- Who are your current key partners?
- Who are our key suppliers?
- Which key resources are supplied by your partners?
- Which key activities do your partners perform?
- If you don't have an alliance/partner, why not?
- Would working with an alliance/partner increase delivery of your Value Proposition?

Why partner?

1. **Optimisation and economical**
2. **Reduction of risk and uncertainty**
3. **Acquisition of specific resources and activities**

It's important to join forces with organisations who share the same core values and beliefs that you do. Make a list of organisations that you feel can benefit from your Value Proposition as well as add value to your business.

Finances

Cost structure

The cost structure relates to the essential costs needed to enable the business to function.

Questions to consider:

- What are the most important inherent costs in your business model?
- Which key resources are most expensive?
- Which key activities are most expensive?
- Is your business cost or value driven?

KEY TERMS

Cost driven: This business focuses on the leanest cost structure possible. This is done by minimising costs as a result of escalating automation systems, extensive outsourcing and using low price Value Proposition. An example of cost driven businesses are supermarkets.

Value driven: This business focuses on the value that they offer their customer segments. The emphasis is on premium products and services and value creation. An example of a value driven business is a chain of luxury hotels.

Characteristics of cost structures

There are four different types of cost structures:

1. **Fixed costs**: These costs remain the same regardless of the quantity of products or services produced, e.g., salaries, office space rental, subscription.

② **Variable costs**: These are variable as a result of the quantity of products or services e.g., credit card transaction fees, direct labour costs, raw materials, commission paid to the sales team.

③ **Economies of scale**: These decrease depending on the amount of goods or services produced, e.g., larger companies that can make large orders benefit from lower bulk purchase rates.

④ **Economies of scope**: Costs decrease as a result of incorporating other businesses which have a direct relation to the original product. In a large enterprise, the same marketing activities or distribution channels may support multiple platforms.

The flow of money is the life blood of the business. It's important that every penny coming in is accounted for and every penny going out is working to propel the business model forward. Seek expert advice and invest in your education so that you can make the best choices possible. It's also important to note that you will still make mistakes, but the scale of each mistake will be minimised if you apply these basics principles.

Revenue streams

The revenue stream defines the source and flow of the business' income.

Questions to consider:

- What value are customers willing to pay?
- What do they currently pay?
- How are they paying?
- How would they prefer to pay?
- How does each revenue stream contribute to overall revenues?

Types of revenue streams:

1 **Asset sale**: Refers to the selling of ownership rights of a physical product, e.g., buying property. This is the most common type of revenue stream.

2 **Usage fee**: Revenue generated through customer using your service, e.g., payments received after using Uber.

3 **Subscription fees**: Revenue generated by customers buying into a continuous service via a subscription, e.g., income generated from Sky subscriptions.

4 **Lending / Leasing / Renting**: Revenue generated through the offering of an exclusive right to an asset for a specific period, e.g., hiring a limo.

5 **Licensing**: Revenue generated from charging for the use of a protected intellectual property, e.g., the use of musical lyrics or songs.

6 **Brokerage fees**: Revenue generated from a fee charged by an agent or agent's company to conduct transactions between two parties, e.g., a broker selling a house for commission.

7 **Advertising**: Revenue generated from fees charged for product and service advertisements, e.g., selling advert space in a newspaper or magazine.

Pricing methods

There are two types of pricing methods:

1 **Fixed pricing**

- List price
- Product feature dependent
- Customer segment dependent
- Volume dependent

② Dynamic pricing

- Negotiation (bargaining)
- Yield management
- Real-time-market

'If your business is not making money, then you are not in business.'

Once you have done all the hard work of identifying your target market, creating a Value Proposition that fulfils your customers' needs and finding a niche, you need to get paid. To ensure your income, you need to closely monitor your customers' buying trends, innovations in technology and new competitors. These are just some of the factors that will have an effect on your bottom line, so stay vigilant and stay ahead of the game.

The BMC is like any tool — in the hands of a novice a masterpiece you will not see. However, in the hands of a master, wonders prevail! To become a master, you will need to keep practicing, refining and implementing what you learn along your entrepreneurial journey. The BMC will help you refine your processes but it's down to you to be disciplined, consistent and committed to your actions.

Activity

Complete your own BMC using the online tool Canvanizer[7]. This will help you craft out a strong business model. In addition, you might want to check out the Value Proposition Canvas. This tool will give you greater insight to your customers' needs and help you create a stronger customer product market fit.

---

7   https://canvanizer.com/

Principle #3: Establish Powerful Metrics

'Statistics are like bikinis.
What they reveal is suggestive, but what they conceal is vital.'
Aaron Levenstein, Business Professor at Baruch College

What are Metrics?

A metric is 'a system or standard of measurement.' A metric's main function is to monitor and gauge the efficiency and effectiveness of a specific business process, performance, progress and quality of an idea or plan. It should be quantitative and qualitative so that the relevant departments can determine how well or not an area is performing. It takes discipline and skill to analyse the data and implement changes based on the results. Ignoring your metrics will stunt the growth of your business.

Why implement metrics?

There are tonnes of metrics you can choose to implement into your business. However, the ones you choose are the ones that will make an immediate impact in your business. So, they have to be the *right* ones for you.

First, it's important to know what makes for a good metric.

The four features of a good metric:

1. **Simple to measure**: Simplicity is key. A good metric should be easy to implement and measure.

2. **Aligned with your business performance**: It's important to align the metric to your business objectives and goals. The right metric will tell you if these are being met.

③ Allow foresight: These are different from financials. Financials tell you how well you are doing *now*, while good metrics tell you how well you *will* do.

④ Take your competitors into account: A good metric should be able to show you how well you are doing in comparison to your competitors. It should provide you with clear data that enables you to analyse the development of your business and the growth and decline of competitors within your industry.

Four essential metrics for your business:

① Sales & Marketing

② Internal Processes

③ Operating productivity

④ Customer retention

Metric 1: Sales & Marketing

Sales and marketing metrics inform you of how effectively your marketing is. The key aspect of this metric is understanding how many units are sold over a defined time period and how this compares to the sales in the same period at an earlier point in time.

Another key aspect of this metric is defining the client's purchasing journey. It's imperative to know where your clients are throughout the cycle. At launch, they are learning about your product or service. Are they still at the discovery and learning stage or are they now considering making a purchase? You need a system in place that tracks and monitors where the clients are sitting on that journey. This type of analysis tells you how successful any marketing campaigns have been, e.g.,

- Who has viewed the advertisement and where

- How the advertisement has been viewed

- The numerical response to a particular advertisement

It's necessary to note that everything that is directly or indirectly related to selling is a revenue metric. Whether it's measuring the effectiveness of a marketing campaign by determining how many products were sold or measuring how many existing customers have been retained, it's vital that you chose the right metrics to measure your company's growth.

Key Metrics for Sales & Marketing

Table 3.1: Key metrics for sales and marketing

Employee satisfaction	Lead to client conversation rate	Referrals acquired
Growth of loyal customers	Revenue growth	Time taken to resolve issues
Qualified leads per week/month	Customer satisfaction	Customer retention rate
ROI* – Total marketing and sales investment	Website traffic and conversion	Length of buying cycle
Open rates of emails, newsletters blogs/vlogs	Campaign performance	Customer acquisition

KEY TERMS

*ROI stands for Return On Investment. To calculate the ROI, you simply take the gain of an investment, subtract the cost of the investment, and divide the total by the cost of the investment.

$$ROI = (Gains - Cost)/Cost$$

Example: *If you buy 50 shares at £10, your investment cost is £500. If you then sell those shares for £650, then your ROI is 0.3. You can also express this as a percentage: 30%.*

List your top three sales and marketing metrics

1 _____

2 _____

3 _____

Metric 2: Internal Processes

Internal Processes (IPs) are the systems that allow you to manage your Business procedures and help streamline and automate the work flows. IPs allow your business to run effectively and efficiently.

Business usually only address the IPs when there is a problem, and often, this involves troubleshooting as opposed to fixing the underlying cause. To avoid this, implementing robust systems from the outset is imperative. These IPs can be reviewed and revised accordingly at intervals appropriate for your type of business. Having effective IPs will put an end to those crisis meetings!

The IP function measures the effort put in and the outcome achieved. You or your department heads must evaluate the results to determine if you are moving towards your goals. The IP should reduce error rates, improve response times and create a culture of efficiency, effectiveness and excellence.

All areas of the business should have an IP manual. The IP manual clearly outlines how an area such as Sales & Marketing, HR, Operations, Branding and Finances etc., should operate, giving you and your team a firm foundation and clear framework that illustrates what needs to be done to achieve your objectives. It will help you refine and improve the systems that you have created, especially as you perform regular reviews to ensure it remains fit for purpose. Do this by scheduling a quarterly meeting for the purpose of reviewing selected IP manuals.

The mindset of the team should always be one that always asks 'how can we simplify and increase standards?' This mindset drives the development and review of IPs and is guided by the *why*, *purpose* and *vision* of the organisation.

There are three IPs that you should be integral to your IP system[8]. They are:

Table 3.2: Three Internal Processes for your business

Internal Process	Customer management	Operational management	Innovation processes
Description	This process enriches your customer value	This process yields and provides your products and services	This process assists the creation of new products and services
Example	Selection, acquisition retention growth	Supply, production and distribution	R&D Design Launch

When you are installing your IPs, aim to automate as many of them as possible so that resources can be directed to other areas and staff can find time to upskill.

---

8   Taken from www.theclci.com/products_pmms-bsc03.html

Metric 3: Operating productivity

Operating productivity is a metric that allows you to measure innovation, efficiency and effectiveness, client experience and control and risk. This metric is very important as it will help you make the necessary adjustments that are needed to refine and realign the business. When implementing this metric, remember these three things:

1 Provide an experience for your customer

As you build a business that engages, excites and elevates your customers, you must be sure to monitor their response to your products and services. It's naïve to think that because your customers have no complaints, they are satisfied. Check in on them at pre-defined intervals relevant to your type of business. Review the collated feedback and use the information to add further value for your customers.

2 Cash is king

Cash flow is the life essence that will ultimately determine if your business has a future, let alone leaves a legacy. Two areas you must pay special attention to are:

- How quickly you are being paid
- How quickly you are paying your suppliers

If you are paying out more than you earn, this is a clear indication that there is a system failure, though it can be easy to fix. It could be that you have outstanding payments from customers and you will need to address this issue as quickly as possible. Alternatively, you may be paying your creditors sooner than you have to, leaving you short. It is very important that you pay what you owe on time but if you have been allocated a window, use this to support your cash flow. It's not about working hard or smart but by working *effectively, efficiently and with excellence.*

③ Support, guide and educate your employees

You should see your employees as customers of the organisation. You are not selling them your product or service but the *vision* and the *why* of the business. If you approach it from this angle then you know you will need to provide an experience for them as well. Find out:

- Which of their personal needs the organisation can meet
- What their career path and educational needs are
- How they feel about change
- How they can contribute to major decisions

Attention to the above will help keep the morale of the organisation high but also keep your employees focused on why they do what they do for the organisation.

Metric 4: Customer retention

Customer retention refers to a business' ability to keep a paying customer over a pre-defined duration of time.

Note that this metric is overlooked by many small businesses in the early years. They understand the importance of branding and marketing to attract new clients but it is equally, if not more important, to retain existing clients. Understanding the Customer Lifetime Value (CLV) is key. The CLV is the projected revenue you expect to gain throughout the duration of a customer's lifetime. This is important as it will help you understand the customer acquisition cost (CAC), i.e., how much you need to spend to acquire new customers.

As the CLV is only a projection of what you could expect from building and maintaining a relationship with your customer, it would be judicious of you to decide how you will maintain a long-lasting relationship with your customers. There is no point spending more money acquiring new customers when just focusing and ensuring that you are serving your existing customers will give you a better return. Below you will find a simplified CLV calculator courtesy of Hubspot[9]:

HOW TO CALCULATE YOUR CLV

When implementing this metric, remember these three things:

Repeat Sales x Average Retention Time = CLV

Example: *Let's look at PureGym. Their average monthly package is £19.99 a month. This is what a new member will pay monthly. On average, people stay with Pure Gym for 24 months (give or take 23 months!)*

£19.99 x 12 months x 2 years = £479.76

This shows the value of one customer to PureGym. It is also important to consider that the calculation does not include any additional merchandise or product/services being purchased by the client, so the figure is just a reflection of the average monthly package. Your customer is worth more to your business if you have additional products/services. You will also need to keep in mind their network (friends, family and colleagues) that will be a source of additional revenue for you. You can now appreciate the full CLV when you consider all these variable factors. The value of your customer is invaluable.

Now that we have established the four key metrics that you should embed within your business, what's next? Ask yourself two questions:

① What's working well?

It is important to assess your business to understand what works well and what doesn't. Revise and revamp IPs for those areas that aren't working

---

9 HubSpot is an inbound marketing and sales platform that helps companies attract visitors, convert leads

well. Marketing campaigns, sales processes, lead generation techniques, upsells, referrals, collections and inventory management are far less time-consuming if systemised as we have discussed under IPs. A great tool to help you understand how to systemise these key areas is the book *The Emyth Revisited* by Michael E Gerber[10].

② Am I doing my best?

You mustn't forget the best metric of all — your past performance. You are your Number 1 competitor. Reviewing your past performances goes a long way in qualifying your achievements and working out what works well and what needs to be refined. Use these reviews to set new targets. Even a target as low as a 2% improvement in a chosen area will make a huge difference to your business. For example, if you improved each of the four metrics by 2%, this leads to an 8% increase in your business. Creating a culture of reviewing your past performances and making necessary changes drives you closer to your goal.

Exercise: The 90-Day Metrics Challenge

The 90-Day Metrics Challenge asks you to record (if you are not doing so already) the four key metrics in your business. The aim is to monitor, measure and refine the activities carried out in each metric. You will need to assess and document what is going well and implement new strategies for tasks that are underperforming.

Let's take marketing for example. Imagine you have a Facebook ad running. By using Facebook Insights, you can monitor and measure the effectiveness of that ad. You can target your advert for many purposes such as sign ups to consultations.

Use the table on the next page to monitor and measure your four key metrics.

---

10 Gerber, M. The Emyth Revisited. (1994). NY. Harper Collins Inc

Table 3.3: Your key metrics

Key Metrics	Current Position	Month 1	Month 2	Month 3
Sales & Marketing				
Internal Processes				
Operating productivity				
Customer retention				

Remember:
'what gets measured gets done.'

Principle #4: Define Your KPIs & Your KVIs

'At Hubspot, we believe sales is a science, and it starts with making sound business decisions based on this data.' Hubspot

At this point, you should have a clear understanding of what metrics are and why they are valuable in business. But the work is not yet done. What good is a unit of measurement without a targeted approach to gathering the data?

This is where Key Performance Indicators (KPI) and Key Value Indicators (KVI) come in. Using KPIs & KVIs will enable you to implement the data. There would be no point having a metric without having a clear plan of what you hope to gain from what you are collecting. Let's walk through what these indicators are first, and what we can do with them.

What is a KPI?

A KPI is 'a quantifiable measure used to evaluate the success of an organisation, employee, etc., in meeting objectives for performance.'[11] There are two types of KPIs:

- High level KPIs
- Low level KPIs

Both are companywide indicators but offer different benefits.

High level KPIs offer a top-down view of the company and reflect on the overall progress of the business. Low level KPIs offer more of a bottom-up view of the business that focuses on progress in different areas of the business such as marketing, sales, customer relations, etc. They also focus more on the efficiency of specific departments and rather processes than the overall enterprise.

11 https://en.oxforddictionaries.com

Why use KPIs?

KPIs are markers used to measure how well a company is meeting its targets. They provide a clear outline of how implemented strategies are contributing to an overall objective.

Imagine you ran an events company and your objective was to increase attendance to a specific event by 50% within a year. You would apply several tactics to achieve this attendance rate. How would you assess the effectiveness of your tactics? What could you measure to tell you what contributed to this progress?

Putting event attendance and revenue to one side, you might measure:

- How effective the marketing strategies were by determining how paying customers heard about the event
- Demographics of customers
- New customers gained per £100 spent on marketing for each individual medium
- How many people rated your event highly

Using KPIs enables you to accurately track the progress of strategies towards an objective or goal. In fact, you could say KPIs break down the journey to your goal into a series of quantifiable measurements with which you can gauge how different factors affect your journey towards these goals.

Limitations of using KPIs

KPIs are great at measuring an array of factors and indicating the performance of a business. However, they don't always allow a company to transform the data into action. This is because they don't account for aspects of the data that are reliant on factors outside of the direct control of the business. This creates the added problem of having to sift through a whole host of data and separate the data related to external factors, e.g., customer retention after the emergence of a new competitor from the data associated with controlled and internal factors such as stock availability and speed of delivery.

Standard KPIs are available but aren't always a good fit for every business. This leads to businesses trying to measure the success of their business model using rigid, broad performance indicators that may not necessarily consider the age of the business and its unique challenges.

A large proportion of businesses that fail to implement the right KPIs do so because they adopt reactive, revenue driven planning techniques (such as creating a *buy one get one free* deal due to lack of sales), or a trial and error approach that does not give a clear indication of precisely why a strategy is succeeding or failing. Simply assuming that an increase in revenue indicates the success of an implemented system is naïve at best and makes it easy to overlook inefficient protocols. In short, a trial and error method to business is reckless and can cause the company to haemorrhage large amounts of funds that could have been better allocated.

KPIs provide a limited insight into the future of your business as they only reflect past performance. The data provided by a KPI is an insight into the success of existing protocols and systems. KVIs, on the other hand, provide a window into the future of the business, the projected growth and the value of all the processes that contribute to this growth. They also provide you with the tools to improve your business, not just a glimpse into the quality of the decisions you made in the past.

What is a KVI?

A KVI is a specific metric that is based on the business. They are built on the basis of a comprehensive self-evaluation of the company and its aims before finding relevant ways to measure the relevant data. This makes them bespoke to the company.

KVIs offer easily actionable insights and arm you with the relevant data to monitor the success of the implemented procedures. Another way of looking at KVIs is through the eyes of the customer. KVIs really look at the interaction between the customer and the company from beginning to end and help to develop and nurture that relationship throughout the customer life cycle.

A good way to assess and implement your system of KVIs is by creating an experience while you are engaged with your customers. For example, if you host an event, your KPIs might tell you how many people came, how they bought their tickets and what marketing campaign produced the best result.

However, your KVIs will look at how you can get these prospective customers to buy into a bundle of value you have created while you have their attention. At your event you could introduce a new product that you not only encourage them to buy, but also fill out a feedback form, rate the product and give referrals. Referrals are a great measure to use in managing your KVI's effectiveness. People only recommend something if they value and benefit from a particular product or service.

So, instead of just focusing on getting more leads, pay attention to the ones you have and create an experience that helps them on their journey. Personalise their message, call them, send gifts and make sure you *wow* them so you stay at the forefront of their minds.

Exercise: Measure the effectiveness of your current KVIs over the next 30 days

This exercise will give you a better understanding of how to implement the right KVIs and how you can measure them. Imagine you are assessing the engagement rate of your website.

THE SCORING SYSTEM

The scoring system is an indication as to how well your current KVI system is operating. It can be adapted in other areas to help your business establish how well it is currently performing. The scoring system starts from *1 = KVI system is non-existent* to *10 = KVI system is adequate*. In essence, 1 is low, 5 is medium and 10 is the highest.

Engagement rate on your website

- *Time on site:* On average, how long does your potential customer spend on your website?

- *Interaction with key buttons:* On average, how many of the features does your potential client view e.g., homepage, packages and basket?

- *Items in basket:* On average, how many of your potential customers add items to the basket?

- *Percentage of items checked out:* On average, how many of your potential customers checkout the items in their basket?

Add up the total score by using the scoring system below.

0 – 10   Current system is totally ineffective and customer engagement is poor.

11 – 20   Current system is inefficient; customers may be spending too little time on the site or are not engaged.

21 – 30   Customers are engaged, they are interacting with the site for a reasonable amount of time and key interactions are happening resulting in a fairly consistent conversion to revenue.

31 – 40   Engagement is excellent. Customers are maintained throughout their lifetime of the journey producing a high conversion to revenue.

How do KVIs Differ from KPIs?

Data-driven approaches like KPIs are beneficial as they use aggregated measurements as a foundation for strategies. Simply having a mass of data at the ready is not be enough for a targeted, tactical approach. This is a limitation of KPIs.

KVIs eliminate the fundamental issue that exists when using just KPIs. By having data that is tailored to areas that need improvement they enable companies to create bespoke metrics to collect only the data they want and need.

In conjunction with KPIs, KVIs allow a company to gauge the contribution of various factors to the core objective, whilst KPIs give a more retrospective view of the success of previously used strategies.

In short, KVIs allow you to take the data a step further, and identify factors that influence your achievement of a specific objective. They also measure the scale of an individual factor's contribution to the progress of your objective and focuses on building a better relationship with your customers.

Is there a list of KPIs and KVIs I can choose from?

There are many KPIs and KVIs to choose from. The best way to choose the right ones for your business is to look at your business vision, goals and objectives and choose the best ones that will bring greater satisfaction to your customers, employees and stakeholders. Take the time to research the best ones for you. Here are some to get you started.

Table 4.1: A variety of KPIs

Marketing	Sales	Financial
Traffic from organic search	Customer turnover rate	Number of budget iterations
Qualified leads per month	Lead to sale conversion rate	Internal audit cycle
Retention rate	Weekly/monthly leads/ prospects	Net profit margin
Average time on page	Monthly sales growth	Operating cash flow

Table 4.2: A variety of KVIs

Human	Business	Growth
Recruitment	Customer experience	Innovation
Relationships	Reviews	Resources
Education and development	Compliance	Brand insistence

How do I align the selected KPIs and KVIs with my goals and objectives?

Here's what you can do:

Think about the projected lifetime of your company and where you want to go.

- What KPIs and KVIs will best measure the processes required to achieve your targets?
- How will you use the data you are gathering to inform future decisions?

Use the four essential metrics from the last chapter and choose the best KPIs and KVIs for each of them. Test measure and refine them for the next 90 days.

1. Sales & Marketing
2. Internal Processes
3. Operating productivity
4. Customer retention

For How Long Should I Measure KPIs and KVIs?

Have you heard of the term 90-day sprint? If you have, great. If not, let me explain.

The business year is broken up into four quarters of about 90 days. By dividing your year you allow yourself room to set achievable objectives and remain focussed. This increases the chances of success. At the end of the book, I will set you a 90-Day Challenge that you can adapt for your business and add your key metrics, KPIs and KVIs.

Here are some examples of KPIs and KVIs. ***Can you guess which is which?***

- Profit
- ROI
- Feedback form

Now that you are armed with knowledge, it's time to create a list of your own KPIs and KVIs.

Grab a pen and some chocolate (or for the health conscious, a piece of fruit…though dark chocolate is good!) if your energy is depleted. You can rest once you have taken your company to new heights with the data management system you are about to create!

Now evaluate your list of KPIs and KVIs. Here are some crucial questions to answer:

- Do they give you an accurate measure of the progress of your objectives and goals?

    _____

- Do they encompass all the processes that contribute to the attainment of your objectives and goals?

    _____

- Are the key factors that affect your objectives and goals covered by your KPIs/KVIs?

    _____

- What are the strengths and weaknesses of your KPIs and KVIs?

    _____

- Do they help you measure the progress of your objectives and goals?

    _____

The KPIs and KVIs you choose to help measure the customer or employee experience, as well as the employee and business, are essential for growth. Test, review and refine your KPIs and KVIs. They can transform the productivity of your business and are fundamental to the foundation that forecasts how your company is going to grow. This means your business productivity has a greater chance of leaving a legacy.

ANSWERS TO KVIs AND KPIs

- Profit (KPI)   • ROI (KPI)   • Feedback forms (KVI)

(8) Principles of Mastering the Basics

Part 2:
Setting New Standards

*'A standard is a rule, a quality, a basis, level, or criterion
that you live by each day, which honors
and is congruent with the real you inside.'*
Derek Mills

Principle #5: Improve Your Time Efficiency

*'Time is a created thing. To say, "I don't have time,"
is like saying, "I don't want to."'* Lao Tzu

Time is one of the most precious commodities we have, yet time and time again, entrepreneurs tell me that they don't have enough of it. The reality is not that we don't have enough time, it's that we fail to use it wisely by prioritising our activities with the time we have to spend.

A fundamental principle that entrepreneurs need to understand is that they must focus on how to *invest* time as opposed to how they *spend* time. Spending time comes with little return on our investment. Think about it. If you saw time as a currency, would you spend as much of it with people, work and activities that would bring you little to no return? When we *invest* time, we are deciding who is best to invest our time in, what work should be prioritised in order to see improved results and what activities we should focus on to get us to that next objective. This approach should also be applied to your personal life. Adopting the attitude of investing time will lead to an improved existence.

An often told tale about the value of time

Imagine a bank that credits your account each morning with £86,400. You can spend it as you wish. However, every evening whatever balance remains is cleared.

What would you do?

Draw out every penny, of course!

Each of us has such a bank. It's called TIME.

Every morning, it credits you with 86,400 seconds. Every night the balance clears and nothing is carried over. No overdraft is allowed. If you fail to use the day's deposits, the loss is yours.

There is no going back. There is no drawing against tomorrow. You must live in the present on today's deposits. Invest it well for true health, happiness and success!

The clock is running. Make the most of today.

To realise the value of one year,
ask a student who has failed their final exam.

To realise the value of one month,
ask the parent of a premature baby.

To realise the value of one week,
ask the editor of a weekly newspaper.

To realise the value of one day,
ask a daily wage laborer who has a large family to feed.

To realise the value of one hour,
ask lovers who are waiting to meet.

To realise the value of one minute,
ask a person who has missed the train, the bus, or a plane.

To realise the value of one second,
ask a person who has survived an accident.

To realise the value of one millisecond,
ask the person who has won a silver medal at the Olympics.

Treasure every moment that you have! And treasure it more because you shared it with someone special, special enough to invest your time in. And remember that time waits for no one.

Author Unknown

The 30-Day Time Challenge

So now that we have illustrated the importance of managing your time, I would like to share with you one of the tools we use to help entrepreneurs just like you understand and evaluate how to do it. By evaluating how many hours you have at your disposal, you can gain a better understanding of what priorities you need to focus on and start to build a strategy that will allow you to invest rather than spend your time.

The Time Grid

The time grid below, is a tool that shows how you use your time and so allows you to redistribute that time to priority areas.

How to use the Time Grid

Each block on the grid represents one hour during your waking hours in each day.

Use the colour-coded key, or create your own, to categorise your activities including a colour code for 'free time.'

Every day, over one week, shade each block of time with the colour of the activity that you carry out during that/those hour/s.

Once you have completed a week, fill in the total free time you have left over in the 'free hours' box of your key.

This free time is what you have available to focus on your priorities. Ultimately, we all want to create more quality time for the things we love. This activity helps you to see how much time you have available and work out what you need to do to properly invest your time.

Go wild when you are colouring in! ☺

Table 5.1: Sample Time Grid

	7-8am	8-9am	9-10am	10-11am	11am-12pm	12-1pm	1-2pm	2-3pm	3-4pm	4-5pm	5-6pm	6-7pm	7-8pm	8-9pm	9-10pm	10-11pm	Free hours
MON																	2
TUE																	2
WED																	2
THU																	2
FRI																	4
SAT																	5
SUN																	8

Key	
	Self-development
	Free hours **25**
	Time with partner/family
	Gym
	Work

Table 5.2: Your Time Grid

	7-8am	8-9am	9-10am	10-11am	11am-12pm	12-1pm	1-2pm	2-3pm	3-4pm	4-5pm	5-6pm	6-7pm	7-8pm	8-9pm	9-10pm	10-11pm	Free hours
MON																	
TUE																	
WED																	
THU																	
FRI																	
SAT																	
SUN																	

Key	
	Free hours

Goal for the week:

_____

☐ *(please tick once completed)*   www.exclusivevisions.co.uk

Principle #6: Create Quality Leads for Your Business

'Lead generation excels when a campaign is looking to capture a piece of factual intelligence that could never be modelled or predicted through profiling and sophisticated propensity algorithms.' **Chris Cunningham**

Here is the truth about creating quality leads for your business. There's no easy way to say this, so I will just say it. Creating quality leads is challenging; it takes work and trial and error to create your system. I say this because there are so many tools and resources out there showing you how to build quality leads and this can be overwhelming. There is no 'one-size-fits-all' system out there but there are some fundamental principles that will allow you to create an effective lead system of attracting and sustaining the leads you acquire.

Visionary, motivational speaker, marketing consultant and bestselling author of *Start with Why*, Simon Sinek stated that 'People don't buy what you do but why you do it.' It's important for you to be able to articulate your story so that your clients can connect with you, the vision of your business and grow with you along the journey.

Whilst it is key to gain new leads for your business, it is also important to turn them into paying customers as well as advocates. A great way to achieve this important task is to implement an effective Customer Relationship Management system (CRM). A CRM system helps you manage your customer's details, tracks each interaction that you have with them, monitors their responses and manages their accounts. Such a system will help to keep you at the forefront of the customer's mind during their lifecycle, offers your customers tailored information and rewards customers for their loyalty. Your CRM system will also help grow and sustain your client database.

How to Create and Sustain Quality Leads

One of the first things entrepreneurs should seek to do is to understand where they can find their customers. This is not an easy task; it takes time and effort but, once mastered, will generate revenue and profits for the business for years to come. It's essential to get new leads. However, the focus should be nurturing and retaining your existing clients. By nurturing and providing value throughout the customers' life cycle, you will develop a meaningful relationship with them. These clients will become your biggest advocates and refer you to others thus, by default, creating new leads.

How do you stay connected to your existing clients? You can provide them with valuable content on a regular basis that includes information on:

- how people are growing and developing within your community
- new innovative tools relevant to their needs
- emerging products and services
- relevant events

70% of buying experiences are based on how the customer feels they are being treated (*McKinsey*[12]): the experience is the key factor that differentiates you from your competitors. If a customer remembers their buying experience with you, they will return.

Part of nurturing relationships is using the existing relationships you have built to ascertain the Customer Acquisition Cost (CAC) of your customers. This is simply understanding how long your customer stays with you, and how much they are worth to your business.

---

12 CRM Analysts Mckinsey and Company www.mckinsey.com

HOW TO CALCULATE YOUR CAC

Total spend / customers = CAC
CAC x 24 months* = Customer Lifetime Value (CLV)
CLV x customers = Revenue
Revenue-total spend = Profit

>   * For this example, 24 months has been used for all the calculations. You
>   can add the time that better represents your business.

Table 6.1: Example: Calculating a CAC

Acquired Method	Total Spend	Customers	CAC	CLV	Revenue	Profit*
FB payperclick	£50	100	£0.50	£12	£1200	£1150
Seminar	£150	50	£3.00	£72	£3600	£3450
PR	£300	30	£10.00	£240	£7200	£6900

>   * Profit: number of customers × CAC. This exercise does not take into
>   account other costs.

A more comprehensive CAC

To work this out, you need to determine the total revenue you have
calculated for each customer.

>   Average order value / 1-repeat purchase rate, or £50 / (1 – 0.1) = £55.56.
>   Subtract your CAC from that, and you get a CLV.

Now you have seen the importance of each customer acquired, you
now know that the acquisition cost is not the only aspect you should be
focusing on. Your acquisition strategy can now be tailored to acquire more
suitable customers.

Three proven methods to gaining quality leads

1 **Networking**

Some so-called business gurus will tell you that you must build an online funnel, get yourself a top ranking on Google and spend hundreds, if not thousands on SEO, Payperclick or other fancy ads. However, in this day and age, we tend to forget the power of face-to-face meets.

Before the tech age, business was always done in person. Networking remains a powerful way to build an automatic connection and rapport with potential clients. I am not suggesting that you abandon your online strategies. They are effective and relevant for this age, and they will certainly save you time. However, you can end up hiding behind social media, neglecting a method that has stood the test of time and still produces results.

Here are three things that will help you to network effectively

- **Research**

There are a plethora of networking events out there, making it easy to end up at events that are not suitable for you and your business. Often many conversations are had, business cards are exchanged, but no real connections are made. So it's really important to research events and choose the most useful ones for you. In your research, note the following:

  ○ Who is the event pitched at?
  ○ Who is the host?
  ○ Who are the speakers?
  ○ Have you seen reviews and coverage of past events?

Being selective and having a clear idea of where you are going will increase your chances of making more meaningful connections.

- ### Don't take your business card!

Wait! Stop! Hear me out! I know what you are thinking:

'I've just printed 250 business cards from Vistaprint and all these business gurus told me that I should have these well-polished cards that stand out.'

Now, let's take a moment and think about this: how many business cards do you have in your house, deep in your drawers or filed away neatly in a place you haven't so much as glanced at in years? Remember, this is all about creating connections with people that you meet and doing things differently. If you meet someone you connect with, swap numbers or connect on LinkedIn straight away. Send a message the next day to remind them of who you are and plan your follow-up. This could be to set up a meeting, discuss a joint venture or simply recommend someone's services. I have made contact with around 95% of people whose number I have taken at networking events and this has led to an increase in sales, leads or new connections.

- ### Actively create connections

If you are at a networking event, really listen to the person you are talking to and assess what they may have to offer that can help you move forward. There is nothing worse than having a business card shoved in your hand and a demand that you call and buy a product that you don't need or want.

In addition, think about what the other person may need and what you can offer to help meet that need. It is imperative that you make sure it is of value to them. My motto is 'always give first.' This can be anything from providing valuable information, offering a recommendation, or even just giving advice. It puts you at an advantage. Not only will you be most likely remembered, but when they require your services they are more likely to contact *you*. Reciprocity is key.

Did you know that 86% of consumers say personalisation plays a role in their purchasing decisions (Infosys[13]). When you are speaking to someone, make it all about them. It does not matter if the conversation lasts 30 seconds or 30 minutes. Make sure you give them your undivided attention. Be someone who will be remembered; the best way to do this is to create a personal connection.

2   Speaking at events

Did you know the average person ranks the fear of public speaking higher than the fear of death?[14] So more people are afraid of speaking in public than they are to die! Now, I'm going to ask you to face your fears and do it anyway (if you are not doing it already).

Public speaking is a powerful way to engage, connect and build rapport with your target audience immediately. It's a great opportunity to be with your target market and interact with them meaningfully. However, speaking is a skill that must be refined. The late, great Dr. Maya Angelou said 'People will forget what you said, people will forget what you did, but people will never forget how you made them feel.'

When you are on stage, don't just sell or reel off what you do. Make sure that you:

- Have a great story and tell it well
- Offer valuable information
- Create a connection and experience
- Make it fun

Speaking engagements can help you create valuable leads and offer you an opportunity to make direct sales on the day. They can also help

---

13 Infosys are an organisation that researches on mobility technologies that will become part of our future. www.infoysys.com
14 Brian Tracey website www.briantracey.com

you to create new products. For example, the more content you can film and repurpose in the form of DVDs, CDs and online trainings, the more products and services you can offer. If this all sounds daunting to you, organisations like Toastmasters[15] can help you develop your speaking skills. Online platforms such as Periscope, Insta Live, Facebook Live and YouTube are excellent places to reach out to your audience through livestreaming and video. If you have not done so already, set up an online platform and start a series with valuable content for your customers. This will help build your credibility.

3 Joint Ventures

It's astonishing to see how many entrepreneurs neglect the opportunity to create joint venture (JV) with established companies who have access to thousands of potential clients. This is usually due to a lack of confidence on the part of the fledgling entrepreneur who feels that approaching a big business should only be done once they are established and thriving. Quite the opposite.

Established companies are more than happy to work with young businesses if they have something of value to offer. For example, currently, being a Black Asian Minority Ethnic (BAME) can actually help you leverage a JV with particular organisations. Many are seeking routes into the BAME community and if you have a track record of working within the community, you already have something to offer. In turn, you may be able to negotiate access to their database. You can display each other's logos at your events, run a feature on them in your newsletter or involve them as a speaker at a networking event that you organise. When contacting organisations for a potential JV, it's important to keep in mind what you want and what you can offer. A JV should benefit all parties involved. Above all, both parties should be aligned along their core values.

---

15 www.toastmasters.org

Exercise

- Name three networking events you plan to attend this month. Include why you want to attend, the date and venue of the event.

  1 _____

  2 _____

  3 _____

- Name three events where you can speak. Contact the organiser.

  1 _____

  2 _____

  3 _____

- Name three organisations you would like to enter into a JV with and initiate the process.

  1 _____

  2 _____

  3 _____

Principle #7: Learn the Basics of Selling Like a Master

'You don't close a sale, you open a relationship
if you want to build a long-term, successful enterprise.'
Patricia Fripp

In life, there are certain principles that if applied will yield results. Take the principle of reciprocity — you get what you give. With this principle, both the act of giving and receiving should be an exchange of equal measure.

As an entrepreneur, you should be providing valuable content on a regular basis. By doing this you will build confidence with your potential clients. When you present any new product, service or programme, they will immediately see the value and significance of your offer. They will be inclined to buy from you because you have given something first. By following this principle, you will see steady results.

Now in the world of entrepreneurship, there is but one fundamental principle of business that if learnt, refined and applied on a regular basis, will produce satisfied customers who become advocates. The end result: exponential growth and longevity of your business. This is:

'The art of selling'

During my travels, I have learnt, developed and refined many of my talents. None has served me as well as this art. Learning how to sell effectively and efficiently has provided a wealth of positive outcomes such as:

- Five promotions in five years whilst working in banking

- Public speaking and opportunities to sell from the stage

- Bringing value and significance to my clients

- Letters from delighted clients years after we did business, telling me how I changed their lives

- Being able to actively listen and connect to people

- Acknowledgement letter from a representative of the Queen recognising my book and work as a business consultant. I had written a letter to Her Royal Majesty informing her of my debut book and my work as a business consultant. I asked if she could take a photo of herself holding my book and send it back to me. Unfortunately, she declined the photo op but sent me a lovely letter of recognition instead and even apologised for the delay! Worth a try! My motto in life and business is **be bold**. What will you do today that is out of your comfort zone?

Sales is not about offloading your product and services to one who is willing to buy. It's an opportunity to provide that something that can enrich another's life.

Before delving into the key principles of selling, you will need to set a goal to educate yourself to the highest level possible that enables you to become a master of sales. This is called *synthesis* and means you have grasped the concept to such a high degree that you can now weave in your own style and method (you have now gained mastery). As you know, being a master does not mean you stop learning. You must still practice to refine your skills.

It's time to get your selling on!

The Seven Rules of Sales

① Build a rapport with your customers

'People don't care how much you know until they know how much you care.' John C Maxwell

If you build meaningful connections with your customers, you will see your sales margin increase. You want your customers to know that you are with them past the point of making a sale. You will gain their trust and respect, and this is priceless.

② Qualify the buyer

Does the buyer need what you have? It's tempting to sell a product or service to a customer who shows interest in what you have. However, a great salesperson qualifies their customer first to ensure the product or service is going to be of value and significance to them. The best way to do this is to apply the active listening technique. This is where you ask key questions that the other party can answer directly. They allow you to drill down to determine if the customer needs what you have. The sales proforma (Appendix 2, page 130) lists questions that you can ask using the active listening technique.

③ Set value and significance

You have assessed and established that your customer will benefit from your product or service. What do you do now? Simple. You allow the customer to create a compelling story (desire) in their head about why they must have what you are selling. This is best achieved through a presentation that highlights the customer's pain points and not the features of the product or service. This means that the customer is reaffirming the value and significance of the sale.

Let's establish one point from the outset. This is not you pulling out a flip board and presenting a generic presentation but instead highlighting to your customer the pain they are facing and the implications if they allow this to continue.

④ Intensify the desire

This takes skill. After active listening, the challenges faced by your customer are now centre stage. Your customer now wants a solution. This is where your skill comes in. However, you don't need to have an air-tight solution. What you must do here is guide your customer to buy into your potential solution.

You can use phrases such as:

You: 'Just so that I've got all the information correct...' (*this shows you were listening*).

List all the problems the customer has identified at this point. (By repeating their problems back to them, you are reaffirming in the customer's mind the importance of solving these challenges).

Customer: 'Yes those are all the issues I am facing.'

This is when you apply the art of selling. You are not there to save the customer but to present a potential solution to their problems.

You: 'Ok. What if (*it's so important to start with this phrase as it postulates to the customer that you might be able to help*) I could help with (*list all problems you can help with*). Is this something that you will find beneficial to you/company?'

8/10 times, they will say yes. The reason why it is not 10/10 times is because of lingering objections.

⑤ Disable lingering objections

Now don't get discouraged, because you followed all the steps correctly: you qualified the customer, built rapport, identified and highlighted the need, relayed all the pain points and the customer has still not committed.

There are two main reasons for this. First, you did not demonstrate the full impact that the pain point could have on the customer's business. Second, the customer wants to buy but is holding onto a negative belief. This is a great opportunity to strengthen the relationship. Let's look at a scenario below to show you how you can do this:

> **Customer:** 'This sounds great, but I can't afford it.'

> **You:** (*You need to apply empathy and active listening*) 'I understand where you are coming from (*pause*) (*Mr/Ms name*). Can I ask you a question? Is the lack of money the only thing holding you back from purchasing the product/service?'

> *At this point, the customer will make one final push on any remaining objections.*

> *If the customer has any more objections you will need to spend time uncovering what may be holding them back. However, if the customer responds:*

> **Customer:** 'No, I just can't afford it.'

> *Happy times! The sale is nearly there.*

> **You:** 'So, suppose I can find a way for you to afford this product. Will you commit/invest today?'

> *At this point the customer should say 'yes.' If not, you may need to reschedule another meeting. There is no need to be pushy as there are other customers who need what you have.*

Once the customer commits, ensure you have a range of financing methods or create further value (add ons), so that the customer sees this as a real opportunity to help with his/her pain point. This could be bonus products or services.

6 Conclude the sale

Remember this is the art of sales and remember that *we do not close*. Why? Because there is still work to be done once you have taken payment. Of course, first, go ahead and take payment. You have done everything right and at this point, all you need to do is find out how the customer would like to pay. You can ask the simple question 'How would you like to pay: cash, debit or bank transfer?'

7 Follow up

This stage is crucial as 68% of customers feel 'buyer's regret' once they have bought something. Think about the last time you made a purchase. It could have been a chocolate bar. You ate it and thought 'I didn't really need that even though it tasted good.'

A simple email within 24 hrs or even a phone call to say thank you for the purchase a week later could stave off the buyer's regret and cement rapport. The customer will remember you because they felt cared for.

I suggest you create a system that allows you to touch base with your customers over the next 6 to 12 months. The Tools and Resources listed on page 111 lists some CRM systems from which you can choose the best one for your business.

Principle #8: Holding Yourself Accountable

*'I learned in an extremely hard way
that the accountability falls with me.'*
Stephen Baldwin

The Benefits of an Accountability Partner

Being an entrepreneur can be lonely but having accountability can counter this. Accountability refers to the state of being held responsible for our actions and outcomes of our vision/goals.

As entrepreneurs, we are enthusiastic about fulfilling our vision and are fuelled by passion, excitement and drive. Whilst all these are integral ingredients to help you leave a great legacy, occasionally we need support from others to help us fulfil that vision.

Having an accountability partner is a great way to work alongside someone who is just as invested in your journey as you are. That person holds you responsible for your commitments and helps you achieve your goals. An accountability partner can also coach you through your journey helping you to set objectives. They push you when you lose momentum or procrastinate, giving you a kick up the ass when you need it most.

Characteristics of an accountability partner

✓ Consistent	✓ Supportive	✓ Professional
✓ Knowledgeable	✓ Reliable	✓ Has Integrity
✓ Committed	✓ Punctual	✓ Resourceful

Communicating with your accountability partner

You and your accountability partner should agree on:

- their roles and responsibilities
- the mode and frequency of communication
- frequency of face to face meetings
- minimum weekly check-ins

Table 8.1: Dos and don'ts of working with an accountability partner

	Do	Don't	Why?
Research your Accountability Partner	✓		You want to ensure that you are choosing someone who can offer you the right support.
			Find out who they have coached before, their track record, supported by testimonies. Ensure they have a good understanding of your field.
Be clear on what you want and need	✓		It is crucial that you are clear on you want and need to develop both yourself and your business. Choose an accountability partner who can help pinpoint the problems you are facing and help you achieve results.
Choose someone who will not tell you what you want to hear		✓	Transparency and honesty is key in this accountability relationship as it is important to hear not what you want to hear but what you *need* to hear in order to grow and develop.

Be committed	✓		Choose objectives and tasks that are going to help move the business forward. Remember, commitment is staying the course long after the emotion and excitement have worn off.
Don't make it all work and no play		✓	It is important to make sure that you reward yourself for you accomplishments along the way. Making it fun and exciting will make it a much more enjoyable experience. Creating rewards gives you something to look forward to. This the art of delayed gratification.
Agree on timelines	✓		Be clear about what you are expected to achieve over the next 90 days / 6 months / 1 year. Objectives and outcomes should be set with achievable deadlines. Ensure you are both in agreement.
Agree on consequences	✓		Whilst we should be rewarding ourselves for achieving objectives and goals, we should also set consequences when we are not meeting our set objectives or commitments. This can be a monetary penalty or forfeit that challenges or pushes you. Consequences keep us motivated and engaged to do better for ourselves.

Accountability agreement form

Appendix 1 on page 129 is an example of an accountability agreement form. Both parties sign this after agreeing on the content. A form like this keeps you committed.

Bringing It All Together

Now that you have grasped the concepts of the eight key principles needed to grow a successful business, I want to ensure that you implement and action each one so that you can see results. How often have you gone to a seminar, watched a motivational clip or read a book and felt all fired up and ready to go? How long was it before you resorted back to your old habits because you failed to apply what you had learnt? Well, I hope this book will break that habit and that you allow it to inspire you into action!

I care about your progress and want you to succeed. So I will leave you with a 90-Day Challenge to help you develop the business acumen needed to fulfil your goals.

The 90-Day Challenge — How Does It Work?

The 90-Day Challenge is designed to help you focus your daily activities towards achieving your chosen goal. Each challenge will help you develop each of the eight key principles.

Use the following table to measure your progress for each principle. To maximise this opportunity I would advise pairing up with another *Master the Basics* reader so you can stay the course together and track each other's progress.

Table i: The 90-Day Challenge

Challenge	What was the result?	Done?
Complete the SHIE Matrix at the beginning and end of each 30-day period		
Complete the Goal Roadmap for your most important project		
Use Canvanizer to create your own business model canvas		
Attend 12 networking events over the next 90 days		
Apply for five speaking engagements		
Read or listen to two books a month and implement the key nuggets		
Find an accountability partner and complete agreement		
Complete the time grid		
Make a list of 10 potential mentors and contact them		
Make a list of 10 potential JV partners and contact them		
Start the Operational Manual for your business		
Set yourself three priorities per day for the next 90 days and complete them		

Challenge	What was the result?	Done?
Find an accountant and complete a financial review		
Sign up to the British and City Business Libraries		
Plan a fun activity		
Choose three things into the Tools and Resources section and implement them into business		
Start writing a book within your chosen field		
Create a plan of action to increase your sales by 15% in the next 90 days		
Review your current metrics and insert the ones that will help increase efficiency in your operations, sales, customer experience and employee satisfaction		
Implement and measure the KPIs and KVIs metrics into your business		
Create a customer experience for your clients e.g., loyalty reward		

'Keep going! The key to this is Discipline, Commitment and Consistency.'

Measuring the Outcome of the 90-Day Challenge

This is great! You have stayed the course, and, at this stage, you should have seen changes in you and your business. This part is very important, as you need to reflect on the progress you have made and refine some areas in order to achieve the next objective.

Evaluate the results and if you have maxed out, meaning you have taken that task as far as you can, replace it with a new task. Examine the challenges you faced in the previous task though and take any learnings forward to the next. Once you have reviewed all the tasks, start again. This is an ongoing process and a great way to keep you and the business anchored to your vision, goals and objectives.

Table ii: The 90-Day Challenge: assessing your results

Activity	Yes / No What was the result?	What adjustments do you need to make?
Have you seen an improvement in your strengths?		
Have your weaknesses improved?		
Did you create a Goal Roadmap?		
Did the BMC help your business?		
Did you make meaning- ful connections at the networking events and what opportunities did you create?		

Activity	Yes / No What was the result?	What adjustments do you need to make?
Did you engage in any speaking events?		
Did you learn and implement a nugget from the books you read?		
Did you find a suitable accountability partner?		
Are you managing your time more effectively and how?		
Do you have a mentor?		
Did you create any JVs?		
How has the operational manual helped your business?		
Have you signed up to the libraries?		
Did you set yourself 3 priorities over the 90 days?		
Did you find an accountant and review your business finances?		

Activity	Yes / No What was the result?	What adjustments do you need to make?
Did you achieve your 3 daily priorities?		
Did you participate in a fun activity?		
Did you choose items from the Tools and Resources section and implement them?		
Have you contacted Daniella from Conscious Dreams Publishing for a free 30min consultation to help you write your book?		
Did you create a plan of action to increase sales?		
Which new metric did you insert into your business?		
Did you implement the core KPIs and KVIs into your business?		
Did you integrate a customer experience system into your business?		

A Final Word

It's not about working *smart or hard*. It's all about working efficiently, effectively and with excellence. You should create a business with an ultimate goal in mind and really that is to sell it. It does not mean you have to sell, but it means that you should create something of value and significance that will outlive you and leave a legacy.

Imagine having a business with automated systems in all the key areas, a clear and attainable vision, that is growing year in and year out. Imagine a business that has mastered the basics and created a sustainable operation.

The only difference between the business you have now and that business you imagine is applying the principles you have learnt after reading this book. Now go out there and create your legacy. Be that phenomenal entrepreneur you were born to be. I look forward to seeing you at the head of the table of success.

Remember,
'Be Exclusively You'

Tools & Resources

Recommended Reading

Other books by Dean Williams

Building the right financial mindset

Money is the life blood of a business and it is important to possess sound financial acumen. *Master the Basics* is all about you building your business using principles that will help you create a sustainable business. To help you build a strong financial foundation, my first book *The Path to Financial Peace* will help you implement the basic principles needed to develop the right financial mindset for your personal and business journey. Use both books to create the world you want to see for you and your legacy.

Other Books

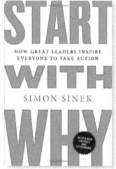

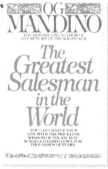

CRM Systems

The description of some of these online resources are as provided on their respective websites.

Salesforce

Salesforce began in 1999 with a vision of reinventing CRM and are known for their pioneering use of cloud computing. Salesforce is a completely integrated solution for managing all interactions with your customers and prospects, designed to help your organisation grow and succeed.

www.salesforce.com

Zoho

Zoho CRM is an award-winning web-based CRM designed to attract, retain and satisfy customers to grow your business. This online CRM software is designed to manage your sales, marketing and support in a single system.

www.zoho.com

Hubspot

Hubspot is an inbound marketing and sales software that helps companies attract visitors, convert leads and close customers.

www.hubspot.com/marketing

Insightly

Insightly, Inc. is a private multinational computer technology company headquartered in San Francisco, California. The company develops cloud-based CRM and project management tools for small and medium size businesses.

www.insightly.com

To explore further CRM software, visit the link below:

Cappterra

www.capterra.com/customer-relationship-management-software

Education

Federation of Small Business (FSB)

FSB offers their members a wide range of vital business services including advice, financial expertise, support and a powerful voice in government. This not-for-profit organisation's mission is to help smaller businesses achieve their ambitions.

www.fsb.org.uk

Institute of Enterprise and Entrepreneurs (IOEE)

The IOEE was founded in 2010, creating the first dedicated professional learning institute specialising in business enterprise and business support.

The Institute's programmes and qualifications are built on the extensive research that underpins the SFEDI® National Occupational Standards and the expertise of the Institute of Enterprise and Entrepreneurs, the UK's only professional institute dedicated to enterprise.

www.ioee.uk

British Library

The British Library is a major research library with items in many languages and in many formats, both print and digital: books, manuscripts, journals, newspapers, magazines, sound and music recordings, videos, play-scripts, patents, databases, maps, stamps, prints and drawings. It has a copy of every publication produced in the UK and Ireland. It's a great place for entrepreneurs to research, develop and study.

www.bl.co.uk

City Business Library

This is a not-for-profit public library specialising in business information, seminars and workshops and meeting room hire, supporting around 50,000 customers each year, 64% of which are businesses ranging from pre start-ups to SME's (small and medium enterprise). They are the only dedicated public library for business information offering free access to the UK's most comprehensive collection of business databases and publications, general start up advice, information on market research, plus national and international coverage for statistics, company data and business news.

www.cityoflondon.gov.uk/business/economic-research-and-information/city-business-library

edX

Founded by Harvard University and MIT in 2012, edX is an online learning destination and massive open online course (MOOC) provider, offering high-quality courses from the world's best universities and institutions to learners everywhere.

www.edx.org

BMC Videos

This is an animated video titled *Getting From Business Idea to Business Model*. Watch the story of Beth, Carl, and an idea they believed could become a great business.

www.tinyurl.com/BMCYoutube

Canvanizer

An online resource to help you develop your own BMC inspired by Alexander Osterwalder to help businesses and teams to brainstorm their ideas. The web tool has easy to share links between team members who are brainstorming on a project, but not necessarily in the same room.

www.canvanizer.com

RSA

The mission of the Royal Society for the encouragement of Arts, Manufactures and Commerce (RSA) is to enrich society through ideas and action.

By sharing powerful ideas and carrying out cutting-edge research, they build networks and opportunities for people to collaborate thus creating fulfilling lives and a flourishing society.

www.thersa.org

Business is Great Britain

This is a free support and advice portal provided by the government. Find the sources of information and practical advice you need to make your new venture a success. Connect to expert advice and sources of information to help you build and grow your business. Use the tools and information resources to plan and drive rapid growth in your enterprise.

www.greatbusiness.gov.uk

GOV. UK

A guide to help companies find the practical support to invest in research and development.

https://www.gov.uk/guidance/research-and-development-in-the-business-sector

Finance

Independent Financial Advisor

Local Financial Advisor Limited is an independent company which acts as an introducer to 'whole of market' independent financial advisors who offer specialist independent financial advice.

www.independent-financial-advisor-uk.com

Start Up Loans

Start Up Loans is a government-backed scheme helping individuals start or grow a business in the UK. Alongside a low-interest loan, successful applicants can access free mentoring from experienced advisors.

www.startuploans.co.uk

Crowdfunder

Crowdfunder is a community of over 600,000 people who are funding the change they want to see. Crowdfunder is a platform that allows you to create your own campaigns to raise money for projects including business ideas, charities, community groups, sports clubs and political movements.

www.crowdfunder.co.uk

Publishing

Conscious Dreams Publishing

An award-winning company that provides bespoke publishing and mentoring services for aspiring authors and entrepreneurs with powerful messages and stories to share with the world. If you are ready to write and publish that book, now is the time!

www.consciousdreamspublishing.com

Public Speaking

Toastmasters

Toastmasters International is a USA-headquartered non-profit educational organisation that operates clubs worldwide for the purpose of helping members improve their communication, public speaking and leadership skills.

www.toastmasters.org

TED

TED is a non-profit devoted to spreading ideas, usually in the form of short, powerful talks. TED began in 1984 as a conference where Technology, Entertainment and Design converged, and today covers almost all topics — from science to business to global issues — in more than 100 languages. Meanwhile, independently run TEDx events help share ideas in communities around the world. To sign up to become a speaker or recommend someone you know visit:

www.ted.com/about/conferences/speaking-at-ted

Online Courses

Udemy

Udemy is a global online learning and teaching marketplace with over 55,000 courses and 15 million students. It is a programme that allows you to become an instructor sharing your knowledge and expertise in your field by building your own course, and a place where students can master new skills and achieve their goals by learning from an extensive library of courses taught by expert instructors.

www.udemy.com

Teachables

Teachables is a powerful yet simple platform that easily helps you share your knowledge and create great interactive online courses.

www.teachable.com

Thinkific

Thinkific brings beautifully simple course creation to your company. Whether you are educating 10 students or 10 million, feel confident that you've got the easiest technology and the best support in the business.

www.thinkific.com

Lead Generation

Thrive Themes

Thrive Themes is the simple-to-use WordPress suite of website tools that allow you to create content, build landing pages and generate leads. They create truly conversion-optimized plug-ins and themes to give a 'real boost to your business.'

www.thrivethemes.com

Wistia

Wistia is a video hosting and analytics company with tons under the surface. With Wistia you can upload your content to the web, make it your own and track how every viewer is watching it. Wistia gives you the power to understand how video is working for your business and how to make it work even harder.

www.wistia.com

Unbounce

With Unbounce Convertables, you can launch targeted overlays on top of any web page, each with a dedicated call to action. Customizable triggers and targeting rules give you complete control over who sees your offers and when, so you can serve the most relevant offers to the right audience.

www.unbounce.com/conversion-rate-optimization/introducing-unbounce-convertables/

Leadpages

Leadpages offers you 350+ high-performing, mobile-responsive landing page templates designed to maximize your conversion rates.

www.leadpages.net

Marketing

Flixpress

Flixpress is pioneering the way toward a new era of media creation. Flixpress allows you to create promotional videos, trailers and short adverts for your business.

www.flixpress.com

Freelance Work

Upwork

Formally known as oDesk, Upwork is an online staffing portal that connects employers to employees whilst in front of their PCs. It is one of the largest marketplace sites in the world which is why it is popular among virtual assistants and other freelance workers. This global marketplace targets businesses that want to hire and manage remote workers.

www.upwork.com

PeoplePerHour

PeoplePerHour is a community of talent available to work for you remotely, online, at the click of a button.

www.peopleperhour.com

Fiverr

Fiverr is a global online marketplace that provides services for companies and freelancers. This portal accommodates the buying and selling of gigs or micro-jobs online. Gigs range from getting a well-designed business card, a career consultant creating an eye-catching resume design, help with HTML, JavaScript and the like. Right now, Fiverr records more than three million different works on the site which start from $5.

www.fiverr.com

FiverUp

FiverUp is another site that allows you to search for freelancers or sell your services.

www.fiverup.com

Networking Events

Eventbrite

An easy to use platform that allows you to set up and create events online, invite people to your event and reach a new audience with promotional tools. Features allow you to check guest lists, scan tickets and throw a great event without a hitch. You can also browse and search for a plethora of events in your field and area of interest.

www.eventbrite.co.uk

Meetup

Meetup brings people together in thousands of cities to do more of what they want to do in life. It is organized around one simple idea: when we get together and do the things that matter to us, we're at our best. And that's what Meetup does. It brings people together to do, explore, teach and learn the things that help them come alive.

www.meetup.com

WeAreTheCity

WeAreTheCity is a free, centralised hub for women that provides news, a networks directory, listing of events and conferences, returnships, business schools, profiles on inspirational women, HeForShe interviews and jobs.

www.wearethecity.com

Motivational Speakers, Mentors and Entrepreneurs

Patrick Bet David

Patrick is passionate about shaping the next generation of leaders by teaching thought-provoking perspectives on entrepreneurship and disrupting the traditional approach to a career.

www.patrickbetdavid.com

John Assaraf

John is one of the leading behavioural and mindset experts in the world with a unique ability to help people break free from the mental and emotional obstacles that prevent them from achieving their very best in life and business.

www.johnassaraf.com

Brad Burton

No one does it quite like Brad. His approach to life, business and motivation is unique. Yet it works. He fires people up from all walks of life giving them permission to do the very thing they know they should be doing. He is Founder of 4Networking and an author.

www.bradburton.biz

Carrie Green

Carrie Green is founder of The Female Entrepreneur Association which is an online hub with the mission of inspiring and empowering women from around the world to turn their ideas into a reality, build successful businesses and live a life they love.

www.femaleentrepreneurassociation.com

Brendon Burchard

Brendon Burchard is the world's leading high performance coach, the most requested motivational speaker of his generation and one of the most-watched, quoted and followed personal development trainers in history. He is also in the Top 100 Most Followed Public Figures on Facebook, with over 10 million fans across his pages, and the star of the web's most shared personal development videos (now over 100 million views).

www.brendon.com

Vonley Joseph

Vonley is the principal at the Bob Etherington Academy. He has spent his life in sales and marketing since starting in sales at the age of 16 back in 1984.

He is committed to seeing sales become a professional career pathway in UK schools, colleges and universities and is one of the founder members for the *Get Britain Selling* campaign and Society of Sales Innovation Cooperative Society.

www.linkedin.com/in/vonleyjoseph

Junior Ogunyemi

Junior coaches and inspires people to become successful entrepreneurs. Whilst at university, he made headlines for launching many successful ventures and became a multi-award-winning business starlet. Due to the remarkable social impact of his success story, a publishing company approached Junior to write a book. At age 21, he became the bestselling author of the highly influential book *How to be a Student Entrepreneur.*

www.juniorogunyemi.com

Tai Lopez

Tai Lopez is an investor, partner, consultant or advisor to over 20 multi-million-dollar businesses. Through his popular book club and podcasts, Tai shares advice on how to achieve health, wealth, love, and happiness with 1.4 million people in 40 countries. Tai started what is now one of the world's largest book clubs that reaches 1.4 million people. He also created an alternative to the traditional business school. This 'Business Mentorship' program combines the best of self-learning with the best of a university degree without the burdens of costs and inefficient methods.

www.tailopez.com

Bianca Miller

Bianca was a contestant in the BBC's *The Apprentice* in 2014 beating 80,000 applicants and 18 candidates to make it to the final where she proposed her concept for *True Skin*. The show culminated in a hotly contested final and in 2015 *Bianca Miller London* was born. Her brand is built on direct enquiries from viewers of the show where the brand proposition was viewed by over 120 million people worldwide.

www.biancamillerlondon.com

Rashada Harry

In a voluntary capacity, Rashada is co-founder of the innovative social enterprise *Your Future, Your Ambition* (YFYA) which inspires children and young adults from diverse backgrounds to study Science, Technology, Engineering and Maths (STEM)-related subjects and pursue careers in STEM-based industries.

www.wearethecity.com/rashada-harry-vodafone

Simone Vincenzi

Simone Vincenzi's purpose is to support individuals to grow successful conscious businesses so they can leave their legacy and make an impact in the world.

She is the co-founder of GTeX (Growing Together eXponentially Ltd), an award-winning speaker, author, life and business purpose expert.

www.gtex.org.uk

Gary V

Gary Vaynerchuk is a serial entrepreneur and the CEO and co-founder of VaynerMedia, a full-service digital agency servicing Fortune 500 clients across the company's 4 locations. Gary is also one of the most sought after public speakers today. He is a venture capitalist, 4-time New York Times bestselling author, and an early investor in companies such as Twitter, Tumblr, Venmo and Uber. Gary has been named to both Crain's and Fortune's 40 Under 40 lists.

www.garyvaynerchuk.com

Business Support Tools

Yammer

Yammer allows cross-company connections to discuss ideas, share updates, and crowdsource answers from co-workers around the globe. Yammer gives your team a faster, smarter way to connect and collaborate across your company.

www.products.office.com/en-us/yammer/yammer-overview

WHYPAY?

WHYPAY? is a catch-free, cost-free conferencing service. Their 03 dial-in number is included in your bundled minutes under Ofcom regulations.

www.whypay.net

Camcard

CamCard captures all your business cards and all the contact information can be quickly & accurately read and saved to your smartphone.

www.camcard.com

Survey Monkey

Survey Monkey design surveys using over 100 expert templates and over 2,500 questions approved by survey scientists.

www.surveymonkey.co.uk

Typeform

Typeform gives respondents a seamless interface for answering survey questions across devices and platforms.

www.typeform.com

Department for Business, Energy & Industrial Strategy

This government service allows you to find tools and guidance for your business as well as information on business finance and grants.

www.gov.uk/government/organisations/department-for-business-energy-and-industrial-strategy

Sniply

Sniply is a simple tool that allows you to overlay your own custom message onto any piece of content, creating an opportunity for you to include a call-to-action with every link you share.

www.snip.ly

Proofing and Editing

Grammarly

Instantly fixes over 400 types of errors, most of which Microsoft Word® can't find. Find the perfect word every time with context-optimized synonym suggestions. Learn about your mistakes so that you can avoid them next time. Whether you're writing emails, essays or social media posts, Grammarly has your back.

www.grammarly.com

Social Media Sites

Facebook

Facebook is an American for-profit social networking site founded by Marc Zuckerberg designed to connect users worldwide. Users can add other users as 'friends', exchange messages, post status updates, share photos, videos and links, use various software applications ('apps') and receive notifications of activity. There are a number of business features too such as public pages, business pages, shops, functionalities as well as Facebook ads.

www.facebook.com

LinkedIn

LinkedIn operates the world's largest professional network on the internet with more than 500 million members in over 200 countries and territories.

www.linkedin.com

Snapchat

Snapchat is an image messaging and multimedia mobile application that allows users to upload brief snapshots of livestreams that last for a short period of time.

www.snapchat.com

Twitter

Twitter connects everyone to what's happening in the world right now. From breaking news and entertainment, to sports and other everyday topics, see what's happening in the world, live, as it unfolds.

www.twitter.com

Google+

Google+ is an internet based social network that is owned and operated by Google. If you have a Google Account, you can activate your Google+ account as easily as you would activate Google Now.

www.plus.google.com/+googleplus

YouTube

YouTube is an American video-sharing site that allows you to share and upload content, videos and music as well as livestream.

www.youtube.com

Instagram

Instagram is a social media platform for images. Users can upload images and use them for visual storytelling, marketing, branding or simply to share photos. Instagram has become the home for visual storytelling for everyone from celebrities, newsrooms and brands, to teens, musicians and anyone with a creative passion.

www.instagram.com

Appendices

Appendix 1: Accountability Agreement Form

As your accountability partner I will ensure that you have:

- A clear and detailed plan
- Start and end date of agreement
- Specific, measurable tasks set each week
- Clear objectives for your vision
- An accountability diary
- Set consequences
- Email and phone support
- 3 face to face meet ups

(Client name) role is to:

- Attend agreed meetings
- Carry out the tasks
- Stay focused on the plan created
- Record progress using the accountability diary

Client signature _____ Date _____

Accountability Partner _____ Date _____

Appendix 2: Sales Proforma

Business Name

Decision Maker

Address

Postcode

Business Telephone Number

Mobile Telephone Number

Email

Website

---

1 How long have you been trading (yrs)?

A 1 to 4   **B** 5 to 10   **C** 11 to 20   **D** 20+

2 Do you have a corporate vision or mission?

A Yes   **B** No

3 What is your vision / mission?

_____

4 What is your current company turnover?

A Under £100,000   **B** £100,000 to 250,000   **C** Over £250,000

5 Do you want to develop your business for growth?

A Yes   **B** No

6 What are the pains in your business right now?

_____

_____

_____

_____

7 What do you think will happen if these issues are not rectified?

_____

_____

_____

_____

8   What is your budget for developing your business?

    A £1,000 to 5,000   **B** £5,001 to 15,000   **C** £30,000+

9   When do you want to develop your business?

    A ASAP   **B** in the next 3 months   **C** in the next 6 months

10   What do you think your business needs to grow?

_____

_____

_____

_____

11   Suppose we are able to help with… (*List issues customer raised that you are able to support*). When would you like to start the process?

_____

_____

_____

_____

_____

_____

_____

_____

Appendix 3: Core Values

The 10 values of Exclusive Visions

1 Passion	**We love what we do** We love what we do for our clientele. Serving others gives us immense fulfilment. We are passionate about quality, efficiency and excellence.
2 Service	**We are specialists in Customer Experience Management** We understand that providing a customer experience is the next level after service. By doing this, we create advocates for our business which will help build our legacy.
3 Vision	**We are visionaries** We do not allow our current status quo to determine what is possible for us; instead we dream and take the steps necessary to make our goals a reality.
4 Integrity	**We do not compromise on integrity and character** We do what we say & say what we do, continuing on the journey long after the emotion and excitement has worn off.
5 Ambition	**We want to be market leaders** We aim to break into the top ten business consultancy companies in the UK and make the overall top ten in the world.

6 Empowerment	**We are empowerneurs**
	We aim to serve, inspire and empower businesses and individuals to reach their goals in the context of love and joy. By doing this we create *empowerneurs.*
7 Excellence	**We want to be the best in our field**
	Like all businesses, we strive to be the best at what we do. We create a culture of excellence and high standards.
8 Education	**We are authentic educators**
	With our expertise, we work with our clients for our clients to successfully build their ultimate business model and strategy.
9 Teamwork	**We build phenomenal teams**
	We understand that Together Everyone Achieves More (TEAM). We invest in individuals who believe in our core values and whose core values complement and enrich Exclusive Visions. Our team understand that their work and achievements must live beyond their lifetime.
10 Legacy	**We help businesses to create a legacy**
	At Exclusive Visions, we help support businesses to grow, develop and leave a legacy for the next generation.

Bibliography

- www.obolinx.com/resources/2012/03/five-performance-metrics-key-to-successful-business-operations/

- www.inc.com/joel-trammell/the-5-characteristics-of-an-effective-business-metric

- www.klipfolio.com/resources/articles/what-are-business-metrics

- www.scoro.com/blog/key-performance-indicators-examples

- www.forbes.com/forbes/welcome/?toURL=https://www.forbes.com/sites/martinzwilling/2011/09/28/10-metrics-every-growing-business-must-keep-an-eye-on/2/&refURL=&referrer=#764c899c5c25

- www.articles.bplans.com/7-key-metrics-every-business-owner-monitor/

- www.ap-institute.com/

- www.yfsmagazine.com/2013/04/27/key-performance-indicators-9-business-metrics-every-startup-should-watch/

- www.shift.newco.co/kvis-and-why-they-are-the-hidden-gem-of-data-intelligence-758b174025e7

- www.a2knowledge.com/blog/using-key-value-indicators/

About Dean Williams

Dean Williams, a former banker, is a business mentor, inspirational speaker, bestselling author and the co-founder of Exclusive Visions.

He is passionate about educating and empowering entrepreneurs using *l*eadership, *o*rganisation, *v*ision and *e*mpowerment to elevate his clients' businesses. For this, he is also known as the L.O.V.E Business Consultant.

As well as writing and providing consultancy services, Dean also runs educational seminars and workshops for entrepreneurs with a focus on creating businesses that become legacies.

Website: www.exclusivevisions.co.uk

Email: info@exclusivevisions.co.uk

Facebook: Dean Williams / Exclusive Visions

Twitter: @DeanExVisions

Skype: dean.williams501

Lightning Source UK Ltd.
Milton Keynes UK
UKHW02f1400280618
324927UK00007B/177/P